The Civil War Letters

of

General

Frank "Bull" Paxton, CSA.

A Lieutenant of Lee & Jackson

The Civil War Letters

of

General

Frank "Bull" Paxton, CSA.

A Lieutenant of Lee & Jackson

EDITED BY
JOHN GALLATIN PAXTON

Introduced by
HAROLD B. SIMPSON

HILL JR. COLLEGE PRESS • HILLSBORO, TEXAS • 1978

COPYRIGHT 1978
HILL JUNIOR COLLEGE PRESS
HILLSBORO, TEXAS

PUBLISHED BY
HILL JUNIOR COLLEGE PRESS

LIBRARY OF CONGRESS CATALOG CARD NUMBER
78-68427

———————————

I.S.B.N.
912172 - 23 - 1

———————————

COMPOSED BY
THE LE-WAY COMPOSING SERVICE, FORT WORTH, TEXAS

PRINTED BY
DAVIS BROS. PUBLISHING CO.
WACO, TEXAS

BOUND BY
THE LIBRARY BINDING COMPANY, WACO, TEXAS

PREFACE

The following is an account of Elisha Franklin Paxton, fellow townsman of Thomas J. (Stonewall) Jackson, both whose paths crossed frequently during the Civil War. The two men left Lexington, Virginia the same week to fight for a cause and each returned during the same week to fight no more during this lifetime.

This story evolves around letters written by Frank Paxton to his wife describing his personal thoughts of the conflict. Credit for collecting and printing them is due to my grandfather's tireless effort that resulted in a small volume entitled, *Elisha Franklin Paxton, Memoir and Memorials,* which was never published.

The history of the Civil War is a tale which will never be fully told and only through personal experiences told by the participants can we ever piece together the complexities of the conflict. It is my hope that the historian may find in this account a name or event that will help him explain to us what happened and why.

General Paxton's letters not only show what manner of man he was and how he thought and felt while a participant in these trying times, but also are representative of his comrades, of whom he was one of the highest types. These letters are a true mirror of the writer, revealing his real qualities of both mind and soul, they explain why he and his comrades were able so long to defend themselves against great odds.

— Dick Paxton
Utopia, Texas

INTRODUCTION

Elijah Franklin "Bull" Paxton was one of the 327 brigadier generals commissioned by the government of the Confederate States of America. He was recommended for brigadier by Stonewall Jackson on September 23, 1862, and was promoted to this rank on the following November 6.

Paxton's claim to fame is that he commanded one of the elite brigades in the Army of Northern Virginia — the Stonewall Brigade — and that he was highly respected as both a man and a commander by Stonewall Jackson. Both men were Presbyterians and both were from Lexington, Virginia. Bull Paxton was the fourth commander of the Stonewall Brigade, following Jackson, Richard B. Garnett (relieved of command after Kerntown), and Charles S. Winder (killed at Cedar Mountain), in that order. Jackson passed over several other colonels who had more combat experience and seniority to give Paxton command of his old brigade. One officer, Colonel Andrew Jackson Grigsby, resigned from the service when Jackson's decision to promote Paxton was made known.

Paxton was born in Rockbridge County, Virginia, on March 4, 1828. One of his first cousins was Elizabeth Paxton Houston, Sam Houston's mother. Thus he and the great Texan were second cousins and both were born in Rockbridge County, Virginia, as was W. A. A. "Big Foot" Wallace, another legendary Texan. Paxton's schooling was extensive. He was graduated from Washington (now Washington and Lee) College in 1845, from Yale University two years later, and then attended Law School at the University of Virginia, where he stood first in his class.

In the early 1850's the strapping Virginian migrated to Ohio to practice law and engage in land speculation. He returned to Virginia in 1854 and opened a law office at Lexington. Failing eyesight forced Paxton to abandon his law practice during the winter of 1860-61, and to pursue the life of a gentleman farmer. He was an ardent secessionist and in the spring of 1861 was elected first lieutenant of Company B (Rockbridge Rifles), 5th Virginia Infantry Regiment. The 5th Virginia Infantry and the 2nd, 4th, 27th and 33rd Virginia Infantry Regiments comprised the Stonewall Brigade.

Bull Paxton fought at the First Battle of Manassas (Bull Run), July 21, 1861. The following month Jackson appointed him an aide-de-camp on his staff. In mid-October, 1861, Paxton received a commission as major of the Twenty-seventh Virginia Infantry; however, he was not re-elected by the men of the regiment when the Brigade was reorganized in June, 1862. Rather than return home, Paxton accepted the position as a volunteer (without pay) Acting Assistant Adjutant General on Jackson's staff. He later became the Chief of Staff of Jackson's Corps. It was while he was assigned to this latter position that Jackson recommended him for brigadier general and commander of the Stonewall Brigade. Paxton commanded the Brigade at the battles of Fredericksburg and Chancellorsville. He was killed at the age of thirty-five leading his men during the second day (May 3, 1863) at Chancellorsville. Paxton was temporarily buried in the yard of the farmhouse near Guiney's Station in which Jackson died. Later his body was moved to the Lexington Cemetery where he was buried a few feet from his old commander. The simple epitaph on his tombstone reads, "It is well with thee."

Some seventy-five letters written to his wife between April 21, 1861, and April 27, 1863, comprise the E. F. Paxton Collection. While some of the material in the letters is of a personal nature, most of the narrative concerns military affairs and warrants publication. The compilation is a most worthwhile addition to Civil War History. As the commander of one of the more famous brigades in Lee's army, Paxton must be considered one of the more important brigadiers in the Confederate Army. His untimely death in battle precluded almost certain advancement to higher rank and at least division command.

Paxton's various assignments during his two year career in the Confederate Army — company officer, division and corps staff officer, and brigade commander — enabled him to view the war from several points of view. These changing points of view are reflected in his letters. He was extremely loyal to Jackson and to the Stonewall Brigade. In his letters he was critical of Jackson only once, for Stonewall's prolongment of the 1861-62 winter campaign. Early in the war Paxton was offered the commission of major by Governor Letcher of Virginia, but refused it so that he could remain in the Brigade.

Paxton's eyesight was poor when the war started and it appeared to be getting worse as time progressed. He complained about this condition in many of his letters, blaming the shortness of the letter on "smarting" eyes. He had a premonition of death. Even in his early letters he mentions death in battle and as the war continued he became more and more obsessed with the idea. Paxton was a devoted Christian, went to church regularly (sometimes with Jackson), encouraged his men to attend the numerous revivals that swept through the Confederate camps in the winter of 1862-63, and in the field was never without his Testament. Just prior to his death in the early morning light of May 3, 1863, Paxton read several passages from the Bible as he awaited the forming of his Brigade. He was a Christian gentleman, a dedicated soldier and a devoted father and husband. His letters bear witness to all these attributes.

— Harold B. Simpson

TABLE OF CONTENTS

ILLUSTRATIONS

CHAPTER I

BACKGROUND OF A CIVILIAN WARRIOR

Elisha Franklin Paxton was born March 4th, 1828 in Rockbridge County, Virginia, the son of Elisha Paxton and Margaret McNutt. His grandfather, William Paxton, came to Rockbridge in its earliest settlement about the year 1745. He was a man of character and substance and commanded a company at the battle of Yorktown. Margaret McNutt was the daughter of Alexander McNutt and Rachel Grigsby. She was one of a family of eight sisters and four brothers, many of whom possessed marked intelligence and great force of character. Alexander Gallatin McNutt, Governor of Mississippi, was one of her brothers. Margaret McNutt Paxton possessed the family characteristics to a high degree. She was a grand-daughter of John Grigsby, whose sobriquet was "Soldier John," going back to his service under Admiral Vernon in his expedition against Cartegena in 1741. He also commanded a company in the Revolutionary War. His soldierly qualities were stamped on his descendants, four of whom were brigadier generals in the Confederate army, and many others were officers of lower rank who followed the Stars and Bars.

The Paxtons were descended from a soldier under Cromwell who emigrated with his Presbyterian comrades to the north of Ireland. As members of a hostile and an alien race their life there was one of conflict. Later they bitterly resented the action of the crown in compelling them to pay tithes for the support of the English Church, and largely on this account emigrated to America. Men like plants take on characteristics from the soil in which they live, the air they breathe and other physical surroundings. These militant churchmen found an appropriate home for the development of their sterling virtues in the beautiful valleys lying between the Blue Ridge and the Alleghenies — the Paxtons in the rough but fertile lands of Rockbridge.

Here on a beautiful spot in the foot-hills of the Blue Ridge, Frank Paxton first saw the light. There in his childhood he imbibed that love of freedom and devotion to duty which marked his ancestors. As a boy he manifested unusual vigor of intellect. He attended the classical school of his cousin James H. Paxton, and at the age of fifteen entered the junior class at Washington College, where he received his degree of A.B. in two years, and afterward took the law course at the University of Virginia. He was five feet ten inches high, heavily built and of great bodily strength. As an indication both of his physical and soldierly qualities he was known both at school and in the army as "Bull Paxton." Doctor John B. Minor wrote the following of his course at the University of Virginia:

> General E. F. Paxton, who fell at the battle of Chancellorsville in May, 1863, was a student of law here, and a graduate in the Law Department of the University in 1849. As a student, none of his contemporaries acquitted themselves more satisfactorily, and in point of conduct, he was entirely exemplary. I think he could then have been not more than twenty one years of age, but I have retained a lively recollection of him during the intervening period of forty three years, so that whilst, after so great a lapse of time, I cannot recall particulars, he left on my mind an impression of unusual merit and a conviction that if he lived, he was destined not only to achieve eminence, but what in my estimation is far better, to attain distinguished usefulness.

Upon his admission to the bar, he spent several years in the prosecution of land claims in the state of Ohio and resided there. He was successful in this enterprise and made some money. In 1854 he opened a law office in Lexington, Virginia, and married Miss Elizabeth White, the daughter of Mathew White of Lexington. This union was a most happy one and there were born of it four children, three of whom survived him — Mathew W. Paxton, John Gallatin Paxton, and Frank Paxton. E. F. Paxton took a high rank in his profession and engaged in important business enterprises, among others becoming the President of the first bank in Rockbridge. His strength of character was shown at this time, when the drinking of whiskey was a universal custom, he abstained altogether from its use, and continued to do so until his death. In 1860 failing eyesight compelled him to abandon his profession and he purchased a beautiful estate near Lexington, known as "Thorn Hill".

In this beautiful home with wife and babes, the drum beat of 1861 found him. It is needless to say that he had been taking an active part in the political events leading up to this. He was a man of intense feeling, when aroused, and had early adopted the view of the Constitution of the United States, which came to him from his fathers. To him the right of secession was as clear as the right of trial by jury. The State was sovereign and in the hot blood of his youth he believed the time had come to secede. So the war in which he entered was for the defense of his home and fireside and against an invading foe. It was as righteous to him as that waged by the Greeks at Thermopylae and his life, if need be, must be cheerfully surrendered in such a cause. In the contest in Rockbridge County over the election of delegates to the secession convention he took an active part in favor of the secession candidates. His great moral courage was conspicuous at the meeting held in Lexington, where he again and again attempted to overcome the large majority opposed to him. He was unsuccessful in this, and Rockbridge sent Union delegates to Richmond.

The county had been a Whig community. During the crisis a majority of the Democrats in the county supported Stephan A. Douglas. A small but vociferous group led by Colonel James W. Massie of Virginia Military Institute and whose numbers included Frank Paxton were for the election of John G. Breckenridge of Kentucky.

The pomp and circumstances of glorious war was present when on that bright spring morning young Frank's company and several others, with colors flying and martial music playing, took up the line of march from Lexington to Harper's Ferry. His young wife with sad forebodings wept until her handkerchief was wet with tears. In their last fond embrace he took it from her hand and as a reminder of her love carried it on many a bloody battlefield.

The above account of Elisha Franklin Paxton was taken from a small volume of letters which was printed but never published by Frank's son, John Gallatin Paxton in 1905. The book was entitled *Memoir and Memorials of Elisha Franklin Paxton.*

CHAPTER II

IT'S GOING TO BE A LARK BOYS

New Market, April 21, 1861

I reached here this morning in good health and in spirits as good as could be expected, considering the bloody prospects ahead and the sad hearts left at home. It is bad enough. I have no time to think of my business at home. My duties now for my State require every energy of mind and body which I can devote to them. Do just as you please. If you think proper stay in town and leave all matters and keys on the farm in charge of John Fitzgerald.

Love, Frank

Thus begins a series of letters which this narrative surrounds. Frank Paxton wrote his wife about war and fear for the future. Events have been included to give the reader an insight of what was taking place while Frank wrote his loving wife.

Upon arriving at Harper's Ferry, Frank found a camp controlled loosely by Virginia Militia. Very little organization was found until Major Jackson arrived. [1]

Harper's Ferry, April 25, 1861

We reached this place on Tuesday morning. Instead of being fatigued, I was rather improved by the trip. Here we have all the comforts which we could expect, good food and comfortable quarters, better than generally falls to a soldiers lot. I have enough to occupy every moment of my time in preparing the company for the service which we may expect to see before long. They have much to learn before they can be relied on for efficiency. I regret that my eyes are no better as it is necessary for me to read much for my own preparation. Try, Love, to make yourself contented and happy. I would not like to think that I was forgotten by dear wife and little ones at home, but it would give me a lighter heart to think that they appreciated the necessity of my absence, and the high importance of a faithful discharge of my present duties. My eyes will not enable me to write more without risk of injury to them.

Love, Frank

A holiday atmosphere prevailed at the camp which included sons of the best Virginia families. Relatives with such names as Randolph, Harrison, Mason, Carter, Beverly, Morgan, Lee, and many others visited the boys. The home folks were impressed with sunset reviews but leadership in camp consisted of political

---

[1] Frank E. Vandiver, *Mighty Stonewall*, p. 136, McGraw-Hill Book Company Inc., New York, 1957. (Hereafter cited as Vandiver)

appointees who regarded war as a lark. Officers had done nothing to prepare the men for an enemy attack.[2]

Harper's Ferry, April 29, 1861

I received your letter by Mr. Campbell and was very happy to hear from you. Nothing could be half so interesting as a line from dear wife and little ones at home. Be cheerful and act upon the motive which made me leave you to risk my life in relieving my State from the peril which menaces her. I hope I may see you again, but if never, my last wish is that you will make our little boys honest, truthful, and useful men. Last Thursday night, I experienced for the first time the feeling of coming in contact with bullets, bayonets, and sabres of our enemies. We were called up suddenly upon the expectation of an engagement which proved a false alarm. Now I know what the feeling is, and know I shall enter the struggle, when it comes, without fear. Next to the honor and safety of my State in her present trial, the happiness of wife and little ones lies nearest my heart. My health was never better. I have spent two nights on duty in the open air without suffering, and feel assured that my health will not suffer by such over exposure.

Kiss the little ones for me and never let them forget "papa gone," perhaps forever. Accept for yourself every wish which a fond husband could bestow upon a devoted wife.

Love, Frank

On April 30th. upon assuming command, Major Thomas J. Jackson began developing an efficient military machine by improving organization and discarding men whom he thought ill-fitted to meet an enemy.[3]

Harper's Ferry, May 4, 1861

Write very often. Nothing can be so interesting to me as your letters. Some of the other wives, you think, get more letters than you do, and you women measure your husband's love by the number and length of their letters.

I will write to you, Love, about once a week and half a page at a time. I cannot with justice to my eyes write longer letters. This will be handed to you by Major Preston, who will tell you everything you want to know. Kiss the children for me, and for yourself take my best love.

Love, Frank

A Confederate War Department personnel order dated May 15, 1861 directed Brigadier General Joseph E. Johnston to take

---

[2]Henry Kyd Douglas, *I Rode With Stonewall*, p. 117, Premier Books, Fawcett World Library, 67 West 44th. St., New York, 36, New York, 1961. (Hereafter cited as Douglas)

[3]The War of The Rebellion: A Compilation of the Official Records of the Union and Confederate Armies, *Series I, Vol. II, p. 787, Washington Printing Office, 1902. (Hereafter cited as O.R.)*

command of the forces in and around Harper's Ferry.[4]

Harper's Ferry, May 18, 1861

My wife, I have no sweeter word than this to call the dear little woman at home, with whom my happiest reminiscences of the past and fondest hopes of the future have ever been associated. (You speak of dreams; I hade one of you, that we were married again, and thought we had a nice time of it.) We have moved from our station in the mountain back to town. Here we have very pleasant quarters, in which I think it likely we will remain until we have a battle. When this will be, it is impossible to say, but it is not expected immediately. I received the green flannel shirt and put it on the first time today. It is very comfortable and valued the more because made [sic] by the hands of my dear wife. Present my kind regards to John [the gardener] and hand him the enclosed order on William White. Present my kindest regards to Jack, Jane, and Phebe [slaves]. Kiss the children for me, and for yourself take a husbands best love.

Love, Frank

The B & O Railroad connected Washington with the west. Jackson controlled the Harper's Ferry and Martinsburg sector of the line which was important if the Federals were to get coal from the west. Stoppage of all traffic would have alienated people in Maryland and West Virginia. The 5th Virginia Regiment was sent by Jackson to Martinsburg to control movements by the many trains traveling east and west.[5]

Martinsburg, May 24, 1861

After mentioning it in your letter, you add a post-script, "Don't forget to tell me where your books are." I told you in my last letter, but wish I had not. Really, Love, I do not wish you to be annoyed with my business. Go out home occasionally and see how matters are going on, but do not trouble yourself any further. So, Love, if any one calls on you about my matters, tell them my instructions to you were to have nothing to do with them. Write no more about business, but about my dear wife and little ones, if you wish to make your letters interesting. We have been kept moving since we came here. We have a hard time, but have gotten used to it. The men were discontented and unmanageable at first, but are now very well satisfied. This section now is in most complete condition for defense, abundantly able, I think to resist any force which can be made against it. Troops have been lately arriving in large numbers. I have no idea when the battle will be fought. Many of us will fall in it, but I have no doubt of our success. And now, my darling, good-bye until I write again.

Love, Frank

---

[4] O.R. II, p. 877.

[5] Colonel G.F.R. Henderson, *Stonewall Jackson and the American Civil War*, p. 92, American Edition, One Volume Edition, Longman, Green And Co., New York, 1961. (Hereafter cited as Henderson)

On May 31st. General Johnston stated, "That this place cannot be held against an enemy who would venture to attack it."[6]

I received your sweet letter of the 1st. inst. on yesterday, and the return of Mr. McClure gives me the opportunity of sending you a line in return for it. When McClure came here to see his son, a member of our company, I offered him my hand, which he took, and thus I have made friends with the only man on earth with whom I was not on speaking terms. I bade a cordial good-bye to Wilson when I left home, which I think he returned in the same spirit of good will. I now may say that there is no one on earth for whom I entertain any thing but feelings of kindness, and I think I have the ill will of no one. In view of the danger before me, it is indeed gratifying to feel that I leave no one who has received a wrong from me which I have not regretted and which is not forgiven. If Mr. McClure calls on you, for my sake treat him with utmost kindness. Send me the miniature.

Good-bye dearest

General Jackson wrote his wife Anna on June 14th., "General Johnston has withdrawn his troops from the heights (Maryland and Virginia), has blown up and burnt the railroad bridges across the Potomac, and is doing the same to the public buildings."[7]

Winchester, June 15, 1861

On Tuesday last we marched on foot from Harper's Ferry to Shepherdstown, thence seven miles farther up the Potomac. There we remained a day and a half, then were ordered to this place, on foot again, and reached here, forty miles, in a day and a half. How long we remain here, or when we move again, I have not an idea. I hardly thought I would have been able to stand forty miles walk so well. Last night I felt very tired, but this evening entirely recovered. The last three nights I have slept in the open air on the ground, and never enjoyed sleep more. I saw Captain Jim White today, and his College boys. Lexington has been well drained of its youth and manhood. I heartily wish, Love, that I was with you again, I hardly know what I would not give for one day with wife and little ones. But I must not think of it. I would soon make myself very unhappy if I suffered my mind to wander in that direction. I ought to be grateful to omnipotence for such a love as that which you gave me. Blood and kindred never made such a stronger tie. We have just received orders to hitch up again — for what destination I do not know. Harper's Ferry has been abandoned by our forces, and here after direct your letters to the address below. Kiss the dear little baby boys for their absent papa, and for yourself accept the best love of a fond husband.

Love, Frank

---

[6] O.R., II, p. 896.
[7] Mrs. Mary Anna Jackson, *Memoirs of Stonewall Jackson*, p. 160, Louisville, 1895. (Hereafter cited as Mrs. Jackson)

Johnston moved quickly on the 16th. of June to meet the Federal force under General George Cadwalader who had crossed the Potomac. Marching westward toward the Martinsburg turnpike near Bunker Hill, Johnston placed his troops in front of the Federal column rushing toward Winchester. Retreating toward the town in advance of the enemy, Johnston "was in position to oppose either McClellan from the west or Patterson from the northwest thus forming a junction with General Beauregard when necessary."[8]

On June 19th., Jackson's Brigade was ordered to destroy all railroad equipment at Martinsburg. The men proceeded to set the torch to the rolling stock of the Baltimore and Ohio Railroad and before they had finished, 305 cars and 42 locomotives were left smoldering. After which they destroyed bridges at Harper's Ferry and Shepherdstown, while ripping the tracks from their crossties.[9]

Camp Stephens, near Martinsburg, June 30

I wrote you last Monday, and was immediately ordered off on another location, in which I have been engaged the greater part of the past week. I was in charge of a small force engaged in destroying a bridge some ten miles from our camp on the railroad. It was a rather dangerous expedition, but I have become so much accustomed to the prospect of danger that it excites no alarm. I thought when we left Winchester that we certainly would have had a battle in a very few days; but two weeks have elapsed, and there is, I think, less reason to expect one now than there has been heretofore. The enemy is encamped on the opposite side of the Potomac some ten miles from here, but, I am satisfied, in less force than we have in this vicinity. Under such circumstances, if we get a fight or shall have to cross the river and make the attack. Our picket-guards occasionally come in contact, and the other day one of the Augusta Cavalry was severely wounded. I hope you are having good success as a farmer; so, if I should be left behind when the war is over, you may be able to take care of yourself. You think, Love, I write very indifferently about it. As to the danger to myself, I am free to confess that I feel perhaps too indifferent. Not so as the separation from loved wife and little ones at home. I never knew what you were worth to me until this war began and the terrible feeling came upon me that I had pressed you to my bosom, perhaps, for the last time. I always keep upon my person the handkerchief which I took from your hand when we separated. It was bathed in tears which that sad moment brought to the eyes of my darling. I will continue to wear it. It may serve as a bandage to staunche [sic] a wound with. I keep one of your letters, which may serve to indicate who I am, where may be found the fond wife who mourns my death. May neither be ever needed to serve such a purpose! Enclosed I send a letter from James Edmonson to his

[8]O.R., II, p. 696.
[9]Lenoir Chambers, *Stonewall Jackson,* Vol. I, William Morrow and Company, New York, 1959. (Hereafter cited as Chambers)

grandmother. Say to Mrs. Chapin that she may rely upon my acting the part of comrade and friend to George. Kiss the children for me, and for yourself accept all that a fond lover and husband can offer.

Frank

The Federal General George Cadwalader received his orders from General Robert Patterson to move on July 1st. and cross the river at Williamsport. At daylight the troops began fording the Potomac and Jackson ordered the 5th. Virginia Regiment to intercept them. The opposing forces met and a skirmish known as the "Affair of Falling Waters" developed causing but few casualties on both sides. Following this engagement Jackson pulled back to Darkesville where he joined forces with Johnston.[10]

Near Winchester, July 8, 1861

The last week has been one of patient waiting for a fight. On Monday, the 1st. inst., I was ordered by Col. Jackson to go to Martinsburg and burn some engines, at which I was engaged until Tuesday morning, when I received an order to join my company, accompanied with the information that the enemy was approaching and our forces had gone out to give him battle. I obtained a conveyance as speedily as I could, and the first intelligence of a fight I received from my regiment, which I found retreating. My company, I was pleased to learn, had fought bravely. On Wednesday morning we took our stand ten miles this side of Martinsburg, and there awaited the approach of the enemy until Sunday morning, when we retired to this place three miles from Winchester. This we expect to be our battle-field. When it will take place is impossible to say. It may be tomorrow, or perhaps not for a month, depending upon the movements of the enemy. I look forward to it without any feeling of alarm. I cannot tell why, but it is so. My fate may be that of Cousin Bob McChesney, of whose death I have but heard. If so, let it be. I die in the discharge of my duty, from which it is neither my wish nor my privilege to shrink. The horse trade was entirely satisfactory. Act in the same way in all matters connected with the farm. Just consider yourself a widow, and in military parlance, insist upon being "obeyed and respected accordingly." Pay your board at Annies out of the first money you get. She may not be disposed to accept it, but I insist upon it. I do not wish to pay such bills merely with gratitude. Newman is still in the army, but I have not seen him for a month. I called to see him the other day, but he was not in his quarters.

It is now nearly three months since I left home, and I hardly know how the time has passed. All I know is that if I do my duty, I have but little leisure. I am used to the hardships of the service, and feel that I have the health and strength to bear any fatigue or exposure. Sometimes, as I lie upon the ground, my face to the sky, I think of Matthew's little verse, "Twinkle, twinkle, little star," and my mind wanders back to the wife and little ones at home. Bless you! If I never return, the wish which lies nearest to my heart is for your

---

[10]Vandiver, p. 151.

happiness. And now, my darling good-bye. Kiss little Matthew and Galla for me, and tell them Papa sends it. Give my love to Pa and Rachel, and for yourself accept all that a fond husband can give.

Frank

—NATIONAL ARCHIVES

GENERAL THOMAS J. "STONEWALL" JACKSON

CHAPTER III

I THINK THE FIGHT
IS OVER FOREVER

Jackson's First Brigade prepared three days rations and marched through Winchester early on the morning of July 18th. The column took a southeastward turn which appeared strange to the men due to Patterson's position lying to the northeast.[1]

An hour after leaving town, Jackson stopped the colum Lining the men in regimental front he read the following from Johnston: "Our gallant army under General Beauregard is now attacked by overwhelming numbers. The commanding general hopes that his troops will step out like men, and make a forced march to save the country."[2]

Jackson's letter to Anna at a later date stated: "The soldiers rent the air with shouts of joy, and all was eagerness and animation where beforehand there had been only lagging and uninterested obedience."[3]

On July 21st, a bloody Sunday, the first battle of Manassas was fought. Later in describing the action of his brigade to a friend Jackson said, "You will find when my report shall be published that the First Brigade was to our army what the Imperial Guard was to Napoleon. Through the blessing of God it met the victorious enemy and turned the fortunes of the day."[4]

More than four hundred eighty of Jackson's three thousand men were killed or wounded in this battle.[5]

Manassas, July 23, 1861

My Darling:
    We spent Sunday last in the sacred work of achieving our nationality and independence. The work was nobly done, and it was the happiest day of my life, our wedding day not excepted. I think the fight is over forever. I received a ball through my shirt sleeves, slightly bruising my arm, and others, whistling "Yankee Doodle" around my head, made fourteen holes through the flag which I carried in the hottest of the fight. It is a miracle that I escaped with my life,

---

[1]Chambers, Vol. I, p. 359.
[2]Mrs. Jackson, p. 175.
[3]Ibid.
[4]Douglas, p. 22.
[5]O.R., II, p. 482.

so many falling dead around me. Buried two of our comrades on the field. God bless my country, my wife and my little ones.

Love, Frank

The following was taken from the Lexington *Gazette* dated August 8, 1861:

It is due to our worthy fellow — citizen, Mr. E. F. Paxton, or rather it is due to the county of Rockbridge, to claim credit for Mr. Paxton's conduct, which he has been too modest to claim for himself. A correspondent of one of the Richmond papers a short time since spoke of a Virginian who had been lost from his company during the fight, and fell in with the Georgia Regiment just as their standard bearer fell. The lost Virginian asked leave to bear the colors. It was granted to him. He bore them bravely. The flag was shot through three times, and the flagstaff was shot off whilst in his hands. But he placed the flag on the Sherman Battery, and our brave men stood up to their colors and took the battery. That lost Virginian was E. F. Paxton of Rockbridge.

Paxton answered the above in the following letter to the Editor of the Lexington *Gazette.*

Camp Harmon, August 24, 1861

I do not merit the compliment paid me in a paragraph contained in a recent number of your paper, which gives me the position of leading a portion of the 4th. Virginia and 7th. Georgia in the charge upon the enemy's batteries. The 4th. Virginia was led by its gallant officers, Col. Preston, Moore, and Kent, and it was by order of Col. Preston, who was the first to reach the battery, that I placed the flag upon it. The 7th. Georgia was led by one whom history will place among the noblest of the brave men whose blood stained the field of Manassas — the lamentable Bartow; when he fell, then by its immediate commander, Col. Gartrell, until he was carried, wounded from the field: and then, until the close of the day, by Major Dunwoodie, the next in command.

If the paragraph means, not leading, but foremost, the compliment is equally unmerited. In the midst of the terrible shower of ball and shell to which we were subjected, and whilst our men, dead and wounded, fell thick and fast around us, my associates in the command of our company, Letcher, Edmonson, and Lewis, were by my side; the dead bodies of my comrades, Fred Davidson and Asbury McClure, attest their gallantry; and the severe wounds which Bowyer, Moodie, Northern, Neff, and P. Davidson carried home show where they were. I witnessed, on the part of our company around me, heroism equal to that of those I have named; but as others whom, in the excitement of the occasion, I do not remember to have seen, did quite as well, I may do injustice to name whom I saw. Compared with the terrible danger to which we were exposed at the time, that seems trifling when, at a later hour and in another part of the field, the flag was placed on some of the guns of the Rhode Island Battery, which the enemy were leaving in rapid retreat, the day being already won, and glories of Manassas achieved.

Again I did not get the flag when Bartow fell, but sometime after, from the color-sergeant of the regiment, who, wounded, was no longer able to bear it.

The work done by Jackson's Brigade and the 7th. Georgia and the credit to which they are entitled is stated in the official report of General McDowell, "The hottest part of the contest was for the possession of the hill with a house on it." Here Jackson and his gallant men fought. Here the work of that memorable Sabbath was finished

Sincerely, Frank Paxton

Statue of General Jackson "Standing Like A Stonewall" on the battlefield of 1st Manassas.

CHAPTER IV

IDLENESS IS WORSE
THAN A DOZEN BATTLES

Manassas, July 26, 1861

I wrote a short note to you on Tuesday advising you of my escape from the battle of Sunday in safety. Matters are now quiet, and no prospect, I think, of another engagement very soon. When I think of the past, and the peril through which it has been my fortune to pass in safety, I am free to admit that I have no desire to participate in another such scene until the cause of my country requires it. Then the danger must be met, cost what it may. How I wish, Love, that I could see you and our little ones again! But for the present I must not think of it. Just as soon as the public service will permit I will be with you. The result of the battle has cast a shade of gloom over many who mourn husband, brother, and child left dead on the field. Of those of our company who went into the thickest of the fight, at least one-half were killed or wounded. Some others escaped danger by sneaking away like cowards. The other companies from our country suffered severely as ours. It seems, Love, an age since I have heard from you. You must write oftener. Why is it that you have not sent the daguerreotype of yourself and the children? Send me, by the first opportunity, another shirt just like that which you last sent me. I will lay that by — as it has a hole through it made by a ball in the battle — as a momento of the glorious day. Do not send me any more clothing until I write for it, as I do not wish more than absolute necessity requires, having no means of carrying it with me.

I wish you would call upon Mrs. J. D. Davidson for me, and say to her she has reason to be proud of her brave boy [Fred]. It was by the heroic services of men like him who have sacrificed their lives that the battle was won. He fell just as he and his comrades were taking possession of a splendid battery of the enemy's cannon, and those who were defending it were flying from the field. And now, Love, good-bye. I think you need have no apprehension about my safety for some weeks at least. It is not probable that we shall have another battle very soon; and if we do, as our brigade was in the thickest of the fight before, we will not be so much exposed again. Give my love to Pa, Rachel, Annie, and all my friends. Kiss our dear little ones for their absent papa, and for yourself accept a husband's best love.

Frank

On the first of August the Brigade marched to a spot east of Centreville about eight miles north of Manassas Junction on the road to Fairfax Courthouse. Due to the invaluable work of the Brigade quartermaster, the area was named Camp Harmon in his honor. The men encamped here for the remainder of the month.

Manassas, August 3, 1861

I reached here last night after spending a day at Staunton. When I reached there I found the militia of Rockbridge, and some of the officers insisted upon my remaining a day to aid them in raising the necessary number of volunteers (270) to have the others disbanded and sent home. I was very glad, indeed, that it was accomplished and the others permitted to return homes and attend their farms. I found, upon reaching Manassas, that our encampment had been removed eight miles from there, in the direction of Alexandria; and after a walk of some three hours I reached here about nine o'clock at night, somewhat fatigued. I do not know what our future operations are to be; but think it probable that we shall remain here for some time in idleness. I am free to confess that I don't like the prospect; without any employment or amusement, the time will pass with me very unpleasantly, and such soldiering, if long continued, I fear, will make most of us very worthless and lazy; perhaps send us home at last idle loafers instead of useful and industrious citizens. Such a result I should regard as more disastrous than a dozen battles. In passing along the road from Manassas, the whole country seemed filled with our troops, and I understand that our encampment extends as far as eight miles this side of Alexandria. I think we have troops enough to defend the country against any force which may be brought against us.

Since this much of my letter was written, Lewis has handed me your note of the 25th. ult. You say you are almost tempted, from my short and far between letters, to think that I do not love you as well as I ought. You are a mean sinner to think so. Just think how hard I fought at Manassas to make you the widow of a dead man or the wife of a live one, and this is all the return my darling wife makes of it. If I was near enough I would hug you to death for such mean-ness. In truth, Love, I may say that I never closed one of my short notes until my eyes began to smart. Sometimes I did not wish to write. When we were for some time on the eve of a battle I did not wish to write lest you might be alarmed for my safety. Until the last month, when danger seemed so threatening, I think I have written once a week. But, Love, when you doubt my affection, you must look to the past, and if the doubt is not dispelled, I can't satisfy you, and you must continue in the delusion that the truest and steadiest feeling my heart has ever known — my love for you — has passed away.

I know, Love, you think I exposed myself too much in the battle. But for such conduct on the part of thousands, the day would have been lost, and our State would now have been in the possession of our enemies. When I think of the result, and the terrible doom from which we are saved, I feel that I could have cheerfully yielded up my life, and have left my wife and little ones draped in mourning to have achieved it. Our future course must be the same, if we expect a like result.

Love, Frank

*　　*　　*　　*　　*　　*

Centreville, August 7, 1861

I have received from General Jackson the appointment to act as his aid, and wish you to send my uniform coat and pants by Rollins, Kahle or some one of our men, whichever comes first. Switzer is just leaving, and I have not time to write more.

Love, Frank

Lack of discipline was proving to be one of the Southernors greatest shortcomings. True, the man from the South was a better marksman than his Northern counterpart but he also maintained an independent attitude that defied his working closely with a disciplined unit.

Understanding this, Jackson determined to instill discipline within his Brigade, began using the present respite to emphasize drill on the parade ground. His men started moving in machine like precision until obedience became automatic. "Every officer and soldier," said the commander, "who is able to do duty ought to be busily engaged in military preparation by hard drilling, in order that, through the blessing of God, we may be victorious in the battles which in His all-wise providence may await us." Jackson neither took leave or furlough nor granted it to others.[1]

Camp Harmon, Manassas, Aug. 18, 1861

I promised in my letter of last Sunday to write to you every Sunday, and I will today, but I ought not, as you have not answered my last. I find abundance of employment in my new position but I like it all the better on this account. The last week has been almost one continuous dreary rain, making soldier life more comfortless than usual. I think I shall quit the use of tobacco altogether, as I am inclined to believe that it injures me. I am very glad that my duties require of me very little writing, for what little I do satisfies me that my eyes have not improved, and that it is not safe to use them much. They pained after the writing which I did last Sunday to William White and yourself. I think we have the prospect of an idle life here for some-time to come. I am free to say I don't like it. I would prefer to move into Maryland for an assault upon Washington and a speedy close of the war. But I suppose those in command know best what should be done.

Love, Frank

*　*　*　*　*　*

Camp Harmon, August　, 1861

I had a chance to show my gallantry last week. I was directed one night to pass a Mr. Pendleton and his party through our line of sentinels. I reached the party about ten o'clock, and found the party consisting of an old gentleman driving the carriage, and in it the wife of his son with three or four children. She told me they were going to stay a mile beyond, with a lady from whom she had a letter, and were on their way to Virginia from Washington. Knowing the difficulty they would have in passing the sentinels of the other camps, I

[1] Henderson, p. 123.

volunteered to accompany them. But when they reached the house where they expected to stay all night I delivered their letter and was told they could not be taken in, as the house was full of sick people, and there was no other house in the village where there was any prospect of getting them in. The only chance then was to take the road and run the chance of getting into a farmhouse or travel all night. I went with them, and succeeded in getting them lodging at a farmhouse three miles further on. She was profuse in her expression of gratitude, and I took leave of them and walked back, four miles to our camp, which I reached about one o'clock, well paid for my trouble in feeling conscious that I had done a good deed.

Love, Frank

* * * * * *

Camp Harmon, September 1, 1861

I wish very much this war was over, and I could be with you again at our home. There you remember, Love, you used to read, last December, to me of the stirring events in South Carolina; but we never dreamed that such a struggle would result as that in which we are now engaged, that the husbands and fathers among our people would be called upon to leave wives and children at home to mourn their absence whilst mingling in such a scene of blood and carnage as that through which we passed on the 21st. of July. But so it is. How little we know of the future and our destiny! Dark as the present is, I indulge the hope it may soon change, and I may be with you again, not for a short visit, but to stay. Whilst such is the fond hope, when I look within my heart I find an immovable purpose to remain until the struggle ends in the establishment of our independence. Can the fond love which I cherish for you and our dear little children be reconciled with such a purpose? If I know myself, such is a fact. But, Love, my eye hurts me. It is sad to think of it, and that it disables me for life. It deprives me of the pleasure of reading for information and pleasure, unfits me for most kinds of business, and deprives me of the means of earning an independent support, which I feel I could do if I had my sight. The present is dark enough, but the future seems darker still, when I think of my return home possibly made bankrupt by the confiscation of my Ohio land, and then without means of earning a support or paying for my farm. I must not think of it now; it will be bad enough when it comes. I ought not to press my weak eye any further. Kiss our dear little ones for me. Speak of me often to them. Never let them forget their "papa gone," who loves them so well.

Love, Frank

* * * * * *

Camp Harmon, Sept. 8, 1861

I will devote to a letter to my loving little wife at home part of this quiet Sunday evening. Sinner as I am, I like to see something to mark the difference between Sunday and week-day. We have no drills on Sunday, and generally two or three sermons in different parts of the camp, which was not so some time since, when everything went on as on every other day. This morning we had a sermon from Bishop Johns, who dined with us, and this afternoon he preaches again. We expect this evening a distinguished visitor, Mrs. Jackson, so we shall have mistress as well as master in the camp. The General went for her to Manassas yesterday evening but returned without her, finding she had gone to Fairfax, where he immediately started in search of her. When she arrives his headquarters, I doubt not, will present much more the appearance of civilization. But before she is here long she will probably be startled with an alarm, false or real, of a fight, which will make her wish she was at home again.

—MEMOIRS OF STONEWALL

MARY ANNA JACKSON, wife of Stonewall Jackson

CHAPTER V

HAD A GOOD VIEW OF THE DOME
OF THE CAPITAL

The Brigade marched to a spot within a mile of Fairfax Courthouse. The 33rd. Virginia Regiment drew picket duty on Munson's Hill lying five miles from the Potomac and at night scouts from the regiment could see lights shining from houses in Washington. [1]

Fairfax Courthouse, September 16, 1861

I did not write my regular Sunday letter to you on yesterday. As usual, after breakfast I left the camp on duty, and did not return until dinner, when, very tired, I slept a couple of hours. Very soon I got orders to leave again for a ride of thirteen miles, and did not get back until bed time. This morning we all left for our new encampment, where all are comfortably quartered.

I received your letter of the 9th. inst. a few days since. Indeed, Love, the perusal of your letters gives me more pleasure than I ever received from any other source. Should I not be happy to know there is someone in the world who loves me so well and looks with such deep interest to my fate? To be with you again is the wish which lies nearest my heart. But the duty to which my life is now devoted must be met without shrinking. Before the war is done many, I fear, must fall, and I may be one of the number. If so, I am resigned to my fate, and I bequeath to you our dear little boys in the full assurance that you will give to my country in them true and useful citizens. I wish, Love, the prospect were brighter, but indeed I see no hope of a speedy end of this bloody contest.

Love Frank

*   *   *   *   *   *

Camp near Fairfax Court House, Sept. 22, 1861

I am indebted to you for much pleasure afforded by your sweet letter of the 16th. inst. I know, Love, my presence is sadly missed at home, but not more than my lonely tent I miss my dear wife and her fond caress. I am sure, too, you are not more eager in your wish for my return, than I am to be with you. But I feel sure you would not have me abandon my post and desert our flag when it needs every arm now in its service for its defense. To return home, all I have to do is to resign my office, a privilege which a man in the ranks does not enjoy. Then your wish and mine is easily fulfilled, but in thus accomplishing it I would go to you dishonored by an exhibition of the want of those

---

[1] Chambers, p. 394.

qualities which alike grace the citizen and the soldier. An imputation of such deficiency of manly virtues I should in times past have resented as an insult. Would you have me merit it now? I think not. My love for you, if no other tie bound me to life, is such that I would not wantonly throw my life away. But my duty must be met, whatever the expense, and I must cling to our cause until the struggle ends in our success or ruin, if my life lasts so long. I trust that I have that obstinacy of resolution which will make my future conform to such sentiments of my duty. Mrs. Jackson took leave of us some days since, as the General was not able to get quarters for her in a house near our present encampment. I rode, between sunset and breakfast next morning, some thirty miles to secure the services of a gentleman to meet her at Manassas to escort her home. In return for this hard night's ride she sent by the General her thanks in the message that she "hoped I might soon see my wife." You hope so too, don't you, Monkey? I was well paid for my trouble in the consciousness of having merited her gratitude.

I stopped at Mr. Newmman's camp the other day to see him, but learned from the Deacon that he was at home and that little Mary was dead. I sympathized deeply with them in the sad bereavement. I learned from the Rev. Dr. Brown, who reached here from Richmond this morning, that he saw Matthew at Gordonsville, on his way here. I suppose he will come to see me when he arrives.

Yesterday I was down the road some ten miles, and, from a hill in the possession of our troops, had a good view of the dome of the Capitol, some five or six miles distant. The city was not visible in consequence of the intervening woods. We were very near, but it will cost us many gallant lives to open the way that short distance. I have no means of knowing, but do not think it probable the effort will be made very soon, if at all. I saw the sentinel of the enemy in the field below me, and about half a mile off, and not far on this side our own sentinels. They occasionally fire at each other. Mrs. Stuart, wife of the Colonel [J.E.B. Stuart] who has charge of our ourpost, stays here with him. Whilst there looking at the Capitol I saw two of his children playing as carelessly as if they were at home. A dangerous place, you will think, for women and children. Remember me to Fitzgerald and his wife, and say that I am very grateful for what they have done for me. And now, Love, I will bid you good-bye again. Kiss little Matthew and Galla for me.

Love, Frank

* * * * * *

Camp near Fairfax C. H., Sept. 28, 1861

I will close a delightful Sunday evening in answering your last letter, received a few days since. I heartily sympathize with you, Love, And our dear little Matthew in your wish for my return. My absence does not press more heavily upon your heart than upon my own. But we must not suffer ourselves to grieve over the necessity which compels our separation. We must bear it in patience, in the hope that when I return we shall love each other all the better for it. I have had the offer from Gov. [John] Letcher of a commission as Major. I was much flattered by the compliment, but declined it, as I would be assigned to duty at Norfolk. Feeling that I was more pleasantly situated and could render more efficient service here, I preferred to remain. I was very much tempted to accept it, from the consideration that it would probably afford me an opportunity of passing by home on my way, but I thought this should not make me deviate from what my judgement as approved my proper course. I replied that I would accept the appointment if assigned to duty in this brigade, but would not leave it for the sake of promotion.

The weather begins to feel like frost, and hereafter we shall, I fear, find a soldier's life rather uncomfortable. Sleeping in the open air or thin tents was comfortable a few weeks since; but when the frost begins to fall freely, and the night air becomes more chilly, lying upon the ground and looking at the stars will not be so pleasant. Then we shall think in earnest of home, warm fires, and soft beds. I think I shall get used to it. I have seen many ups and downs and begin to fancy that I can bear almost anything. In November I suppose we shall find comfortable winter quarters somewhere, or shall build log cabins and stay here. I went down to see Mat some days since, but did not find him.

Jim Holly came this evening and tells me he has the pair of pants which you sent me, and that Waltz will bring some more things for me. You need not get the overcoat; my coat for the present answers a very good purpose, and if I find hereafter that I need an overcoat, I will send to Richmond for it.

And now, Love, as I have taxed my eye about enough, I will bid you good-bye. I trust that you will make yourself contented. I shall be all the happier knowing that you are so. Give a kiss to our little boys for me; for yourself accept a fond husband's best love.

Love, Frank

*   *   *   *   *   *

Camp near Fairfax Courthouse, Oct. 6, 1861

Your letter of October 1st. was received on yesterday, and I am very much gratified at the cheerful feeling which it manifests. It shows, too, that you are giving a very commendable attention to the business under your charge, and give promise, if the war lasts, of your being a first rate business woman. You have your mind set in the right direction, for it seems as if the war would be interminable, and the sooner you learn how to take care of yourself the better it will be. Times are very dull with us here. Our troops are but a mile or so distant from the enemy, — so near that our pickets, it is said, occasionally meet and converse with theirs, swap newspapers, tobacco, whiskey, etc. Judging from the newspapers, one would think we were on the eve of a battle every day, but there seems little apprehension of it. We may have a battle, but then again we may not. On the whole, the soldiers would just as lief [sic] fight as not. We are going to have a sermon this evening, and I will bid you good-bye to listen to it. Kiss our dear little boys for me, and remind them of me. I shall regard their forgetting me as the saddest loss sustained by my absence from home. Think of me often, Love, My fondest hope, the dearest wish of my heart, is to be with you again. Remember me to the servants, and to Fitz and his wife, to Annie, Rachel and my friends.

Love, Frank

*   *   *   *   *   *

I have received your last letter, and will devote an hour of this quiet Sabbath to giving you one in return for it. I am very sorry to hear that, having spared your team so long, they have called for it at last. I had hoped they would let it alone in consideration of my absence from home in the service of the State, and consequently my inability to provide means of supplying its place, as others who have remained in the country can. It is nearly equivalent to a loss of our wheat crop, besides the great injury the horses must sustain in such a trip. For them I feel a sort of attachment, as for everything else at home, and should hate very much to see them injured.

We are having a very quiet and dull time. The fault I have with my present position is that I have too little to do. Jackson has been promoted again, and is now Major General. It is, indeed, very gratifying to see him appreciated so highly and promoted so rapidly. It is all well merited. We have, I think, no better man or better officer in the army. I do not know to what position he will be assigned. But this brigade will part with him with very much regret. I shall be very reluctant to leave my place on his staff for any other position.

I am sorry to inform you on the money question that I am dead broke, and gratified to say that I do not expect it to continue many days. I have about $300 pay due me from the government, and sent by a friend who went to Richmond a few days since to draw the money, but he has not returned. Say to Mrs. Fuller I see Sam frequently and he is very well. Kiss the children for me, and think of me often.

Love, Frank

The reorganization of the Confederate Army of Northern Virginia placed General Joseph E. Johnston in charge of the department and headquartered with the Army of Northern Virginia under the command of General Beauregard. General Jackson assumed command of the Valley troops and immediately set up his headquarters at Winchester.[2]

After receiving his promotion, Jackson told his pastor, the Reverend W. S. White, who was with him when he received the post that, "Had this communication not come as an order, I should instantly have declined it and continued in command of my brave old Brigade."[3]

Centerville, Virginia, Oct. 20, 1861

Letters prompted by an affectionate anxiety for my fate, bringing intelligence that wife and children are happy in the enjoyment of every necessary comfort at home, furnish in their perusal the happiest moments of the strange life I am leading. Such interchanges of letters are a poor substitute for the happiness which we have found in each other in times past; but it is all we can have now. Our separation must

---

[2]Douglas, p. 25.

[3]R. L. Dabney, *Life and Campaigns of Lieut.-Gen. Thomas J. Jackson,* p. 435, New York, 1866. (Hereafter cited as Dabney)

continue until this sad war runs its course and terminates, as it must some day, in peace. Then I trust we may pass what remains of life together, loving each other all the better from a recollection of the sadness we have felt from the separation. I am sometimes reminded of you, and the strong tie which binds me to you, by odd circumstances. The other day I saw an officer, who, like myself, has left wife and children at home, riding by the camp, with another woman on horseback, from a pleasure excursion up the road; and I could not help feeling that in seeking pleasure in such a source he was proving himself false to the holiest feeling and the highest obligation which is known on earth. I thought if I had acted thus faithless to you and our marriage vow, I should feel through life a sense of baseness and degradation from which no repentance or reparation should bring relief. If I know myself, I would not exchange the sweet communion with my absent wife, enjoyed through the recollections of the past and the hopes of the future, for any temporary pleasure which another might offer. I would rather love over again in memory the scenes of seven long years, when we talked of our love and our future, our ride to Staunton on our wedding-day, and our association since then, chequered here and there with events of sadness and sorrow, than accept any enjoyment which ill-timed passion might prompt me to seek from another. I trust, Love, this feeling may grow with every day which passes, and that I may always have the satisfaction of knowing my devotion and fidelity merit the affection which your warm heart lavishes upon me.

I have received a commission as Major in the 27th. Regiment, and expect to change my quarters to-morrow. I leave my present position with much reluctance.

Love, Frank.

During the 4th. of November Jackson made a speech to the men assembled en masse in which he said,

Officers and men of the First Brigade, I am not here to make a speech but to say farewell. I first met you at Harper's Ferry in the commencement of the war, and I can-not take leave of you without giving expression to my admiration of your conduct from that day to this, whether on the march, in the bivouac, the tented field, or on the bloody plains of Manassas, where you gained the well-deserved reputation of having decided the fate of the battle. Throughout the broad extent of country over which you have marched, by your respect for the rights and property of citizens, you have shown that you were soldiers not only to defend, but able and willing both to defend and protect. You have already gained a brilliant and deservedly high reputation throughout the army and the whole Confederacy, and I trust in the future by your own deeds on the field, and by the assistance of the same Kind Providence who has heretofore favored our case, that you will gain more victories, and add additional lustre to the reputation you now enjoy. You have already gained a proud position in the history of this Second War of Independence. I shall look with great anxiety to your future movements, and I trust whenever I shall hear of the First Brigade on the field of battle it will be of still nobler deed achieved and higher reputation won.

He waited to catch his breath and continued,

In the Army of the Shenandoah you were the First Brigade; in the Army of the Potomac you were the First Brigade; in the Second Corps of this army you are the First Brigade; you are the First Brigade in the affections of your General; and I hope by your future deeds and bearing you will be handed down to posterity as the First Brigade in our Second War of Independence. Farewell![4]

—CONFEDERATE MUSEUM

Men of the Stonewall Brigade on the march in the winter of 1861-62.

---

[4]Douglas, p. 26.

CHAPTER VI

A KISS TO THE CHILDREN
AS MY CHRISTMAS GIFT

On November 8th., 1861 an order was given by General Johnston directing the 1st. Brigade to move by rail to Winchester.[1]

Camp near Winchester, November 17, 1861

Soldiering for the past week has been a hard business. For two or three days we had cold rains, and the balance of the time very severe winds. The wind is perhaps more severe than the rain, as it makes our outdoor fires very uncomfortable, it being doubtful whether it is best to stand the cold or the smoke. The weather feels now as if the campaign was over and we must soon go into winter quarters. If we get houses, I presume it will be shanties, such as the men can build for themselves out of logs and clapboards. This they could do in a very short time. But cotton tents will be bad quarters for snowy, freezing weather; and if we do not have better, I fear we shall lose much from disease this winter. My health at present is very good, and I think I can stand the service as well as any one else in it. Last night I slept very comfortably with the assistance of two sheepskins and five blankets.

Since our arrival here, there has been a very general congregation of officers' wives at the farm-houses in the neighborhood, and I think it likely to continue until women and children are as common in the camp as black-berries in August. So I have little hope of seeing you here, but think the Yankees will go into winter quarters before long. They will discover that a winter campaign in this part of the sunny South, with the snow a foot deep and ice everywhere is uncomfortable, and will give us a few months' rest. I hope then to be able to get a short furlough to see my dear little wife and babies at home.

And, now, Love, I will take leave of you. I sympathize deeply with you in your approaching illness, and hope for your safe and speedy recovery. Remember me kindly to your father, and say that I am very grateful for the assistance which he has given you in my absence.

Love, Frank

*　　*　　*　　*　　*　　*

Winchester, November 24, 1861

I have read over again this morning your last two letters, and whilst they inspire a feeling of happiness that there is a dear wife at

---

[1] O.R., V, p. 944.

home whose love I prize and cherish more than anything else on earth, yet they make me feel sad that she is unhappy. I think, Love, I take a very calm and just view of my duty and of the future. I think I should remain in the war so long as my services may be needed, although it be at the sacrifice of personal comfort and pecuniary interest, and compels a separation from the loved wife with whom the happiest recollections of the past and the fondest hopes of the future are inseparably connected. It will cost me all this, and perhaps my life. If so, I will but share the fate of thousands who must fall in the contest, doing that which their own judgement and the common sentiment of the country decide to be their duty. If I survive the end of the war, I shall then quit the service, I trust, with the good opinion of my comrades and with my own approval of the fidelity and efficiency with which my duty has been discharged. Poverty and want may then mark my path through life, but I do not expect it, and I do not fear it. I have a strong faith in my capacity to earn a livelihood anywhere, — industry meets its reward, — and to secure every comfort which may be necessary for the happiness of the wife and little ones who bless my home with their presence. Here I'll change the subject to say that while writing our postman has arrived with your letter of 20th inst. I really think, Love, you are doing finely, and your providence in procuring salt in advance of the rise in the market exhibits qualities to fill the place of a soldier's wife which need only a little necessity for developing them. I am glad, too, to hear you say you are too busy to be lonesome; that is a step in the right direction. That is the reason why I was sorry to give up the place of road overseer at Manassas. It gave me abundant employment for mind and body, made me sleep well and eat well. Now I have a job as member of a court martial which requires me to go to Winchester every day, where the court is in session from 9 A.M. to 3 P.M.

Love, Frank

* * * * * *

Winchester, December 1, 1861

I have received your last letter, and am sorry that you write so despondently of the future. It would be sad, indeed, for me to think that day would ever come when the dear wife and little ones whose happiness and comfort have been the chief aim of my life, should be dependent. You would not be more grieved, I am sure, than I would be at such a prospect, and its reality could not distress you more than it would me, if I should be alive to witness it. But, Love, it does not become either of us to harass ourselves with trouble which the future has in store for us. Mine at present is not blessed with as many comforts as I have seen in times past; but it is the case with many thousands who feel impelled with a sense of patriotism and duty to bear in patience, and I shall try to follow their example. When I sent the message to your father I knew that what he would have to give you out of his estate would be abundant to furnish a comfortable support for you and your children, whatever misfortune may befall my life or my property, and I desired, if it had not been done, that it might be secured to you as your own. The widow and orphan of many a gallant man destined to fall before this struggle ends, though deserving, have not, I apprehend, such a prospect of a comfortable provision as you have. So, Love, the best consolation I can offer you is that there are others whose future is as dark as yours, and that yours is not so bad that it might be worse. It grieves me, I am sure, as much as it does you, and we must both make up our minds, as the surest guaranty of happiness, to bear the present in patience and cheerfulness, and cherish a hope of another time, when we shall be together again, loving and happy as we used to be. If I survive this war, I have no fear of being unable to earn, by my own industry and energy, a comfortable support for my household. If fate determines that I must perish in this contest, then I trust that He whose supreme wisdom and goodness tempers the wind to the shorn lamb will shield from want the widow and orphans left dependent upon His providence. This is the first day of winter, and as yet we have had no snow. It has for some time been quite cold, and the water often frozen over. I have not as yet suffered much from exposure, and think I shall stand the winter well. With the assistance of four or five blankets, and bed made of some hay and leaves laid on split timber raised off the ground, I sleep quite warm. I hear nothing said of winter quarters, for the weather and the roads will soon be such as to make active operations utterly impracticable.

Will Lewis and Annie left here Wednesday, I think, and, I suppose, have reached home before this time. I sent by her my likeness and some candy for the children. When he returns send me your likeness — that which was taken before we were married. I suppose you know where it is put away, for I don't remember.

And now, Love, as I have written you quite a long letter compared with what I generally write, I will bid you good-bye till my next. You have my heartfelt sympathy in your approaching illness, and my sincere hope of your speedy and safe recovery. Kiss dear little Matthew and Galla for me, and tell them to be good boys. And now, dearest, again good-bye.

Love, Frank

On December 4th. Major General Thomas Jackson reported that,

On the evening of the 4th. Lt. Col. [Turner] Ashby, who in command of a detachment of some cavalry and an infantry force under Major E. F. Paxton, and a working party under Captain R. T. Colston, had been enlarging the break in Dam. No. 5, joined me at Bath. From the most reliable information received the forces of the enemy at Bath was 1500 cavalry and infantry, with two pieces of artillery.[2]

Jackson began worrying about the Union recruits receiving adequate training in Washington. Although these men had been lacking in discipline and self confidence in summer they were developing into a trained unit by November. He believed that an expedition to the northwest might draw out the Federal forces before they were completely prepared for battle. By occupying

[2]O.R., V, p. 392.

the town of Romney, Jackson would control the railroab hub thus dominating the whole area.[3]

Col. William B. Taliferro's Brigade of the Army of the Northwest on December 8th. marched into Winchester to reinforce Jackson's troops.[4]

Martinsburg, December 9, 1861

I did not write my accustomed Sunday letter to you on yesterday. I was otherwise busy until 9:30 o'clock last night, when I reached here. Then I was so sleepy and awake all the night before, and hard at work most of it. Yesterday I spent on the bank of the Potomac, not as decent people generally spend the Sabbath, in peace and rest, but listening to the music of cannon and musket, and witnessing their work of destruction. There was much firing, but little damage on either side, as the river intervened, and the men of the enemy, as well as our own, were well sheltered from fire. Our loss, I learn, is one mortally wounded and two very seriously; one of the latter is the son of Shanklin McClure of our county, and a member of the Rockbridge Artillery. The purpose of the expedition was to destroy a dam across the Potomac which feeds the canal now used by the enemy in shipping coal. I was appointed to superintend and direct the execution of the work, with some men detailed to do it. We reached the ground about sunset on Saturday evening, when a few shots from our artillery drove off the force of the enemy stationed on the opposite side. I then took down my force and put it to work and continued until about eleven o'clock, when we were surprised by a fire from the enemy on the opposite side again, which made it impossible to proceed until they could be driven away. At daybreak Sunday morning our cannon opened fire upon them again, but they were so sheltered in the canal — from which in the meantime they had drawn off the water — that it was found impossible to dislodge them. As my workmen could not be protected against the enemy's fire, I found it necessary to abandon the enterprise. So you see, Love, entrusted with an important work, I have made a failure. If I had succeeded, the Yankees would have suffered much in Washington for want of coal. But they must get it as usual, for which they may thank their riflemen, who drove my party from the work of destruction upon which they were engaged.

I begin to think, Love, there is no amount of fatigue, exposure and starvation which I cannot stand. I got notice on Thursday about three o'clock that I was wanted at Jackson's headquarters; there I got my directions, and rode here in a hard trot of about six miles to the hour. The next afternoon I rode up and took a view of the work which I had in contemplation and returned here. On Saturday morning we left here with our forces to accomplish it. On Sunday at twelve o'clock I could not help but remark that I felt fresh, although I had not slept the night before, and had nothing to eat since Saturday morning at breakfast, with the exception of a small piece of bread, and had been upon my feet, or my horse, nearly the whole time. I

---

[3]Vandiver, p. 180.
[4]O.R., V, p. 389.

think this war will give me a stock of good health which will last a good while. And now, Love, whilst I have been in the perils of minie-balls, I expect, when I get to Winchester, to receive a letter from somebody saying that you have been in worse perils, and that we have an addition to our small stock of children. The only special message I have is that its name may be yours or mine, just as you like. Whilst, Love, I have just been expressing my gratification at my good health, and my capacity for fatigue and exposure, I cannot help feeling this war is an uncertain life, and there is no telling that you and I may never see much of each other again. I shall try and get a leave of absence to go home this winter; but I suppose it will not be possible until after Christmas, as I think Col. [John] Echols has the promise of a leave at that time, and it would not be proper for us both to be away at the same time.

How much I wish that I was with you, that I could stay at home! But to turn my back upon our cause, to leave the fatigue, patriotism and risk of life which it requires to be borne by others, when duty and patriotism require that I should share it, I cannot do.

Love, Frank

*   *   *   *   *   *

Unger's Store, December 10, 1861

I made application yesterday for leave of absence, but was informed that I could not get it until Col. Echols returned, who has leave for twenty-five days and starts home this morning. It is to me a sad disappointment, but I must bear it as cheerfully as I can. You must do the same. You must make up your mind, too, Love, to stay at home. In the present state of our finances we must save all we can, and this, I feel sure, will be best done by your staying on the farm. I think, too, you will be as happy there as you could be elsewhere.

Love, Frank

*   *   *   *   *   *

Winchester, December 12, 1861

Last Monday night I returned to our camp here, where I had the pleasure of reading the letters of Mary and Helen informing me that your troubles were all over, that we had another little boy in the crib, and that his mamma, as Mary happily expressed it, "Was doing as well as could be expected." I would have written them to express my gratification at the good news from home, but I had orders to leave again upon another expedition to the Potomac which afforded no time for writing a letter. I reached Charlestown the next morning about daylight and spent most of the day on my horse. The morning started with the forces at one o'clock, passing by Shepherdstown to Dam No. 4 on the Potomac, where we captured eight Federal soldiers whom we found on this side of the river, in which we lost one man wounded — I suppose fatally. We remained there until late in the evening, when we started for Martinsburg, where we arrived about nine o'clock, having made a march of about twenty-six miles. I left Martinsburg the next afternoon and returned to Winchester, where, having been some time engaged in a conference with Jackson, I found a bed and went to sleep, tired enough, I am sure. This morning I returned to camp. So, Love, I have given you together my operations for the last few days, which furnish the reason for my not writing sooner.

To-day I received Mary's letter of the 9th inst., from which I learn that you are improving, that the baby is doing well, which I am delighted to hear. I really sympathize with you, Love, in your lonely situation. You must be uncomfortable, lying all day and night in bed, though not suffering much with pain. In ten days more, I suppose, you will be able to sit up, and then in a week or so get about, attending to matters at home, as usual. I assure you that I reciprocate your wish for my return home, and heartily wish that I could consistently with my duty remain with you. If I can get a leave for only a few days, I will go before long to give a kiss and a greeting to the little fellow who has such strong claims upon my love and care. Active operations must soon cease, when there will be no reason why a short furlough could not be granted. The weather is already cold enough to make it uncomfortable in tents and such conveniences as we are able to provide. It would be intolerable if we were put upon the march with insufficient means which the men would have of making themselves comfortable.

I suppose by this time the hands have been making considerable progress in getting up the corn crop, and hope they may be able to finish it before Christmas. For the hired hands clothing must be furnished before Christmas. Can you get Annie or your ma to call upon Wm. White and get the goods and have them made up? Give my love to Helen and Mary and say to them I am much indebted to them for their letters and wish them to continue to write until you are able. And now, Love, good-bye again. Give my love to your father, ma and Annie. A kiss to Mathew, Galla and the baby, and for yourself, dearest, my hearty wish for your speedy recovery.

Love, Frank

* * * * * *

Winchester, December 15, 1861

Life in camp is generally dull with me, and I feel especially dull to-day. I have sometimes had a job, such as road-making at Centreville or my late excursion to the Potomac, which kept me busy enough; but these only happen now and then, and but for them my life would be idle enough, I am sure. When here in camp it really seems that I have no way of employing myself. I sometimes think I would prefer a more active campaign, winter as it is. With my stock of bed clothes I think I could sleep quite comfortably even at this season in a fence corner, but it would not be comfortable to the soldiers, who are not so well provided with such means of a comfortable night's rest. If the weather continues open and the cold not too severe, I think it possible we may have some activity in our operations this winter. But of this no one can speak with any certainty but Jackson, and even he with but little, as his operations depend upon contingencies over which he has no control.

I sometimes look to the future with much despondency. I think most of our volunteers will quit the service when their year expires, and the news I get from Rockbridge gives me but little reason to hope that many more will volunteer to fill the places thus made vacant in our army. If they come at all, I fear it will be by compulsion. I fear there are more who are disposed to speculate off our present troubles, and turn them into pecuniary profit, than there are to sacrifice personal comfort and pecuniary interest and risk life itself for the promotion of our cause. My judgement dictates to me to pursue the path which I believe to be right, and to trust that the good deed may meet its just reward. Nothing else could induce me to bear this separation from my darling wife and dear little children. This distresses me. I care nothing for the exposure and hardships of the service. But, Love, I should be more cheerful, and if sometimes oppressed with a feeling of sadness, should try to suppress it from you; for I should try and detract noting from your happiness, which I fear I do in writing in so sad a strain.

And now, Love, good-bye. I shall be glad indeed to hear that you are out of your bed, and happier still to know, by a letter in your familiar hand, that you are nearly well and out of danger. When the winter sets in so cold that there can be no possible use for my services here, I shall try and get leave to spend a week with you at home. I don't think that snow can keep off much longer.

Love, Frank

Sniping stopped the attempt to break the canal at Dam No. 5 and on December 17th. Jackson took a larger force to accomplish the mission. By the 21st. he decided that the canal had been sufficiently immobilized which prompted him and his men to return to Winchester.[5]

Winchester, December 22, 1861

We left here, on an expedition to the Potomac, on last Monday morning at seven o'clock, and returned again this evening. We lost one man, Joshua Parks, killed by the enemy; and his body, I suppose, has by this time reached his friends in Lexington to whom it was sent for burial. Present my kind regard to Mrs. Parks, and say to her that I heartily sympathize in the sad bereavement which has fallen upon her. He was a brave and good man, universally esteemed and beloved by his comrades, and his loss is much deplored.

Whilst gone we slept without our tents four nights. I had plenty of blankets, and slept as sound as if I had been in quarters. I really could not have thought I could stand so much exposure with so little inconvenience. I think, if my health continues to improve under such outdoor life, I will soon be able to stand anything but ball and shell. I received Helen's letter, for which give her my thanks. I was delighted to hear that our baby is well and growing, and that you are improving rapidly. I am much gratified, too, at your pressing invitation to come home. I believe, Love, you must want to see me. It has been my purpose to ask for a furlough as soon as winter had fairly set in so as to render active operations impracticable. To-day was very cold, — so cold that we all had to get off our horses and make the greater part of the march on foot. To-night we have sleet and snow, which, I think, will pass for winter, especially as it now wants only three days of Christmas. So, Love, I shall ask for a furlough some time this week,

[5]Chambers, p. 182.

and, if I can get it, will be off for home. And if you hear a loud rap at the door some night before long, you need not think robbers are breaking in, but that your own dear husband is coming home to see wife and little ones, dearer to him than everything on earth. But, Love, you must not calculate with too much certainty on seeing me. If I can get the leave I will, but that is not a certainty.

I hope you all may have a happy Christmas, and wish I had the means of sending some nuts and candy for Matthew and Galla. Many who spent last Christmas with wife and children at home will be missing this time — perhaps to join the happy group in merry Christmas never again. But let us be hopeful — at least share the effort to merit fulfillment and fruition of the hopes we cherish so fondly. Now, dearest, good-bye til I see you again, or write. A kiss to the children as my Christmas gift.

Love, Frank

Jackson had been pressing the War Department for more men. By Christmas day he knew that there were to be none prompting him to begin his march to Bath and Romney as soon as practicable.[6]

Winchester, December 26, 1861

I applied to-day for a furlough, but was much disappointed to find that an order has been made that none shall be granted. I was promising myself much happiness in spending a few days with you at New Year's, and am much grieved that it has to be deferred — I hope, however, not very long. I will come as soon as I can get permission. Fair weather cannot last much longer, and winter must soon set in, which will stop active operations, and then I suppose I can get leave to go home for a while. I will make this note short so as to try and get it in to-day's mail. Your box just came to hand as I left the camp this morning, for which accept many thanks. Good-bye, dearest.

Love, Frank

* * * * * *

Winchester, December 29, 1861

The weather opened this morning cloudy and showing signs of snow, but, much to my disappointment, the clouds have passed off leaving a clear sky and pleasant day. It is not often I wish for bad weather, but when it opens a way for me of getting home for a little while I bid it a hearty welcome. It troubled me less when there was no prospect of getting a leave of absence and no use of asking it; but as I have been so anxiously indulging the hope of late, it troubles me much to have it deferred. If the bright sunshine of to-day is destined to last, you need not expect me, for Jackson is not disposed to lie idle when there is an opportunity to win laurels for himself and render service to our cause. The arrival of our forces from the West under Loring has given him a very fine army, which I think he is disposed to turn to a very profitable use as soon as an occasion may offer itself. I have much reason to be gratified at the proofs of his good opinion

[6]O.R., V, p. 1005.

and confidence which I am continually receiving from him. I can rely upon his influence and efforts for my promotion, but my ambition does not run in that direction. The sympathies of my heart and my aspirations for the future are all absorbed in the wife and little ones left at home, and my highest ambition is to spend my life there in peace and quiet. The hope of winning military titles and distinction could not tempt me to leave home, if I were left to consult my wishes and feelings alone. But the sense of public duty which prompts us, and the strong public sentiment which forces us, to leave our families for the public service, now with equal force compels us to remain. If we left the army now, it would be at the sacrifice of such good opinion as we have of ourselves and the good opinion entertained of us by our neighbors and friends at home. Our term of service will expire in May, when each will be left to pursue for himself such course as duty and inclination may then determine. It is sad, indeed, to think of being a stranger in my own home, that wife and children are becoming used to my absence and forced by it to seek other sources of happiness than that which we used to have when the society of each other was the greatest source of enjoyment. When separation so long protracted it seems akin to that which lasts forever, when the body has gone to its long home in the grave and the soul for weal or woe to eternity, when the loved left behind to mourn our loss are no longer left a hope, and after a while become used to the desolation which death has left them. But hope whispers, Love, that all may yet be well with us. The storm may pass away, and, living happily together in after years, it will be a source of pride and happiness to us that the duty patriotism exacts of me now has been faithfully discharged, and the pleasure and comfort of home for the time foregone.

I wrote you a long business letter on Friday, in which you will think, no doubt, I have marked out work enough to keep you employed next year. You will be too busy to think of me and the troubles which this war is bringing on us. Now, darling, as my half sheet is finished I will bid you good-bye. Kiss my three little baby boys for me, and send me your likeness — the old one which I used to have — by the first person who comes from Lexington.

Love, Frank

CHAPTER VII

HARD WEATHER
IS WORSE THAN BATTLE

The 1st. of January, 1862 found Jackson's men on the road to Bath, Virginia where they stayed several days then journeyed back to Unger's Store and thence moved toward Romney. The expedition was plagued by a rash of rain, snow, sleet and storm that was in such contrast with the sunny day in which they had departed from Winchester.[1]

Steadily worsening on the 4th., the men were peppered with snow and sleet while their feet became numb as they tramped through the snow drifts. Men began falling out of line as the temperature lowered.

Turner Ashby and a detachment of cavalry accompanied by an infantry force under Frank Paxton and a working party commanded by Captain Colston continued destruction of Dam No. 5.

Jackson was determined to destroy the Federal waterways on the Potomac.[2]

While trudging toward Ungers Store the men were caught in an ice storm. They slipped on the ground causing rifles to be fired accidentally which startled the horses. Due to helplessness by these horses, the men had to unharness some of the animals and take their place in pulling wagons, guns, and ambulances.[3]

Morgan County, January 8, 1862

An opportunity of sending to Winchester enables me to write that I am here in the woods, all hands froze up and waiting for the weather to move. I take it for granted the General [Jackson] will come to the conclusion from this experiment that a winter campaign won't pay, and will put us into winter quarters. I am quite well and have not suffered much.

Love, Frank

* * * * * *

Camp near Unger's Store, Morgan Co., Va.
January 11, 1862

His Excellency John Letcher, Governor of Virginia.
I hereby tender my resignation of the office of Major in the active

---

[1]Douglas, p. 33.
[2]Chambers, p. 423.
[3]Ibid., p. 424.

volunteer forces of the State conferred by your commission bearing the date October 14, 1861. My private affairs have been brought to such condition of embarrassment by the loss of valuable property which I owned in Ohio, that my personal attention to them, for a time at least, is made my duty by a just regard for the claims of my creditors and my family. If other forces are called into the service of the State, to supply the place of those whose terms of service expire in a few months, I shall be glad to have the offer of such position as your Excellency may think me competent to fill with advantage to the public service.

Respectfully
E. F. Paxton
Major 27th. Regt., Va. Vols.

Endorsements on Resignation.

Camp near Unger's Store, January 12, 1862

Resignation of Major E. F. Paxton, 27 Va. Vols. Approved and forwarded.

A. J. Grigsby
Lt.-Col. Commanding 27th. Va. Vol.

Respectfully forwarded.

R. B. Garnett,
Brig.-Gen'l Comdg.

Headquarters Valley District
Unger's Store, Morgan Co.

Respectfully forwarded, but disapproved.

T. J. Jackson,
Maj.-Gen'l Comdg.

Hdqrs. Centreville, January 20, 1862.

Respectfully forwarded.

J. E. Johnston,
General

Recd. A. O. I., January 22, 1862

Respectfully returned disapproved by the order of the Secy. of War.

R. H. Milton,
A. A. G.

Unger's Store, January 12, 1862

I was much disappointed in not getting a furlough a few days ago. I could not help but think that as the condition of the weather and the roads had made the expedition from which we had just returned a failure, it was full time to stop active operations, and in that event I was entitled to a leave of absence, if they were to be granted to any. I applied and was informed that two field officers must be left with the regiment, and that as a leave had been given to Col. Echols, none could be given to me until he returned. Hardly two days elapsed, however, until I received an order detaching me from my regiment and assigning me to duties of a provost-marshal of the post, thus leaving but one field officer to my regiment. I have handed in my resignation, and whether that will be accepted or not I do not know. Jackson entered his disapproval of its acceptance, which will probably induce the Secretary of War and the Governor to do the same. The disapproval, it is true, implies the compliment that my services are valued, and that those in authority do not wish to dispense with them; but I do not feel satisfied, and the whole affair gives me much unhappiness. I shall endeavor to take such course as will not forfeit the good opinion which I have enjoyed from those with whom I have served, and at the same time try to be content with whatever may happen. I wish you to act upon the same principle. Some of us have as hard a road to travel as yourself. I should like to be at home, and know that you fondly desire my return. If I can't get home, we must both be satisfied. I wish you to make up your mind to remain there, and take care of what we have as well as you can. You have, I doubt not, been as happy there for the last four or five months as you could have been elsewhere. With the work on the farm, your housekeeping, and the children, you will have too much to do to be lonesome. Plenty of work is a good antidote for loneliness; a very good means of drowning your sorrows. By this course you will be of infinite service to me, and will add much to your own comfort and happiness.

If there is an honorable road to get home, I shall spare no effort to find it as speedily as possible. In the meantime, Love, devote yourself to the babies and the farm, and not to grieving about me or my troubles. I will give them my undivided attention and get through with them as soon as I can. I don't wish to share so great a luxury with you. Now, Love, good-bye. Kiss our dear little baby and tell Mathew and Galla papa says they must be good boys. Remember me kindly to Jack, Jane and Phebe [slaves]. I am grateful to them for their fidelity. Tell Jane to get married whenever she wishes, and not to trouble herself about the threats of her last husband.

Love, Frank

* * * * * *

Unger's Store, January 12, 1862

Gov. John Letcher, Richmond, Va.

Dear Sir:

My resignation, forwarded through the regular channel, will reach you in a few days. When it comes to hand you will treat it as withdrawn. I feel much aggrieved by my inability to get a furlough, and by an unjust discrimination made against me in withholding it, whilst granted to others. I have come to the conclusion that it is my duty as a citizen and a soldier to bear the grievance in patience, in the hope that hereafter I may be able to get such furlough as will save me the necessity of quitting the service.

Respectfully,
E. F. Paxton
Major 27th Regt., Va. Vols.

*   *   *   *   *   *

Romney, January 19, 1862

We left Unger's Monday morning and reached here on Wednesday, after three days' hard march on roads as bad as rain, sleet and snow could make them. For some time since we reached here it has been raining, and the whole country is flooded with water. Since we left Winchester three weeks ago, we have indeed been making war upon the elements, and our men have stood an amount of hardship and exposure which I would not have thought was possible had I not witnessed it. In passing through it all, I have suffered but little, and my health is now as good as it ever was. Whilst this is true of myself, our ranks had been made thinner by disease since we left Winchester. Two battles would not have done us as much injury as hard weather and exposure have effected. After writing to you last Sunday, I concluded to write to the Governor to consider my resignation as withdrawn and I would trust to the chance of getting a furlough to go home. I am promised it as soon as Echols returns, and his furlough is out sixteen days from this time. I hope Jackson will have concluded by that time that a winter campaign is fruitful of disaster only, as it has been, and will put us at rest until spring. Then I may expect to see you.

Now, darling, just here the mail has come to hand, bringing your letter of the 15th inst. and the gratifying news that all are well at home. You say the sleet and snow were falling whilst you wrote, and you felt some anxiety lest I might be exposed to it. You were just about right. I left that morning at daybreak and marched in sleet and snow some fifteen miles to this place. When I got here the cape of my overcoat was a sheet of ice. If you have hard times, you may console yourself by knowing that I have hard times, too. I am amused with your fears of an inroad of the Yankees into Rockbridge. Their nearest force is about eighty miles from you, and if the roads in that section have not improved very much, they will have a hard road to travel. You all are easily scared. By the time you had been near the Yankees as long as I have, you would not be so easily frightened.

You must come to the conclusion which has forced itself upon me some time since. Bear the present in patience, and hope for the best. If it turns out bad, console ourselves with the reflection that it is no worse. We can see nothing of the future, and it is well for us we don't. I have but little idea to-day where I will sleep to-night, or what shall be doing to-morrow. Our business is all uncertainties. I have been in great danger only once since I have been in service, yet I suppose I have thought a hundred times that we were on the eve of a battle which might terminate my life. Now, after all, Love, I think it best to trouble myself little with fears of danger, and to find happiness in the hope that you and I and our dear children will one day live together again happily and in peace. It may be, dearest, this hope will never be realized, yet I will cherish it as my greatest source of happiness, to be abandoned only when my flowing blood and failing breath shall teach me that I have seen the last of earth. All may yet be well with us.

Love, Frank

On January 23rd. Jackson moved out of Romney leaving General Loring to hold the town and on the 25th. eleven officers of Loring's command headed by Colonel [William B.] Taliaferro signed a petition directed to the War Department telling of the cruel experiences they had received for which they held Jackson directly responsible.[4]

Winchester, January 26, 1862

We left Romney on Thursday, and after three days we reached, on yesterday evening, our present encampment, two miles from Winchester. To-day I received your grumbling letter of 21st, in which you were bitter over my bad usage in being refused a furlough. The only matter of surprise with me is that I ever lost my temper about it, as I came to the conclusion long ago that there was no use in grumbling about anything in the army, and it was always best to bear in patience whatever happens to us, with a becoming sense of gratitude that it is no worse. I think we shall remain at rest here until spring, no one being more thoroughly disgusted with a winter campaign than Jackson himself from the fruits of our expedition to Romney. Echols' furlough expires nine days hence, and then, I think, I may safely promise myself the happiness of a visit home to enjoy for a while the loved society of wife and little ones, from whom I have been so long separated. For a while only, Love, as my duty will require me to leave you soon again. I wish to pursue such a course as will give me hereafter a good opinion of myself and the good opinion of my neighbors, and neither is to be won by shrinking from the dangers and hardships of a soldier's life when the safety of his country requires him to endure them. But for this, the titles and appluase to be won by gallantry upon the field could never tempt me from home. Would you have me return there the subject of such conversation as has been freely lavished upon those who remained behind and others who turned their backs on country and comrades? I think not.

I don't think Love, you would know me if you could see me just now. I think I am dirtier than I ever was before, and may be lousy besides. I have not changed clothes for two weeks, and my pants have a hole in each leg nearly big enough for a dog to creep through. I have been promising myself the luxury of soap and water all over and a change of clothes today, but the wind blows so hard and cold I really think I should freeze in the operation. I am afraid the dirt is striking in, as I am somewhat afflicted with the baby's complaint — a pain under the apron. I am not much afraid of it, however, as I succeeded in getting down a good dinner, which with me is generally a sign of pretty fair health. Now, Love, I will bid you good-bye, as it is very

[4]O.R., V, p. 1040-1, and 1046-7.

cold and uncomfortable writing, leaving the last side of my sheet unwritten.

Love, Frank

January 27, 1862

Yesterday I concluded after writing this, to come to town and get comfortable quarters, as I felt much inclined to chill. I slept pretty well last night, and this morning am not suffering any pain. I hope to be well in the course of a few days. Should I get worse, I will write to-morrow.

Love, Frank

For several days Paxton continued ill at Winchester, and this perhaps hastened the granting of the greatly desired furlough.

Jackson received the following:

Richmond Virginia, January 30, 1862

General T. J. Jackson, Winchester, Va.

Our news indicates that a movement is being made to cut off General Loring's command. Order him back to Winchester immediately.

J. P. Benjamin
Secretary of war[5]

This made Jackson so angry that he sent a letter of resignation to the Secretary. Jackson also wrote his old friend from Lexington, Governor Letcher, concerning the case. Through action by the Governor and others, they persuaded Jackson to retain command of his troops.[6]

Jackson's Romney trip had been successful. The enemy had been chased across the Potomac and their line of supply had been cut for a while. Jackson captured many stores and a few prisoners and only lost 4 killed and 28 wounded.[7]

---

[5]Ibid., V, p. 1053.
[6]Ibid., V, p. 1058.
[7]Henderson, p. 148.

CHAPTER VIII

DON'T BE ALARMED
AT ANY RUMORS YOU MAY HEAR

Winchester, February 28, 1862

I reached here day before yesterday, and expected to devote yesterday evening to a letter home; but so soon as I got pen and paper ready to commence we had an order to change our camp. My ride here was as pleasant as I could expect. The first night I stayed at Mr. Sproul's, the next at Dr. Crawford's, the next at Mr. Williamson's, and the last at Strasburg, reaching Winchester about twelve o'clock. Self and horse both in good condition.

I doubt not you will hear any quantity of news before this reaches you: that Winchester has been evacuated, the enemy approaching in countless numbers from all directions, and Jackson's army flying before him. All I can say is, do not be alarmed, and make up your mind to bear in patience whatever of good or evil the future may have in store for us. Try, so far as possible, to divert your mind from the troubles of the country. The future is not so bright as it was before our late disasters, but we have yet many strong arms and brave hearts in the field, and should not despair.

As to our situation here, place no confidence in the rumors which you may hear. The enemy yesterday entered Charlestown — in what force I do not know, or for what purpose. It may be to take possession of the Baltimore & Ohio R. R. and rebuild it, or it may be a part of a force intended to advance on this place. All I can say is: I think, unless his force largely outnumbers ours, we shall fight him, and if it is overpowering we shall evacuate the place.

I write, darling, in the open air and a freezing wind, and will bid you good-bye until my next. I will write regularly, so that my letters may reach you Sunday morning when you go to church. Should anything happen to me, I will have a letter written to your father, who will send it to you. Kiss the children for me, and for yourself, dearest, accept all that a fond husband can offer.

Love, Frank

*   *   *   *   *   *

Winchester, March 6, 1862

Your first letter since I left home reached me on yesterday, bringing the welcome intelligence that you were all well, and the intelligence, not less gratifying, that you would not have me stay at home whilst the country has such a pressing need for the service of every citizen in the field. If such were the feeling and wish of every woman and child, the men would be moved by nobler impulses and we would have a brighter prospect before us. Our soldiers, impelled by influence from home, would all remain in the service, and those left behind would rally to their support, instead of remaining behind until compelled by force to join the army and fight for the liberties of the country. Whatever others may do, their delinquencies will not justify our faults; and you and I must act so that what we do in these times of peril and uncertainty shall hereafter have our own and the approval of those whose good opinion we value.

We came to our present encampment a week ago, and have made little preparation for comfort, not knowing how soon, but expecting every day, we might move again. I doubt not you have heard frequent rumors that a battle was imminent. You had best never alarm yourself with such. From this to the end of the war, I never expect to see the time when a battle may not occur in a few days. Hence I always try to be ready for it, expecting it as something through which I must pass, which is not to be avoided. The facts, so far as I can learn, are that the enemy is in the Charlestown area with considerable force, in Martinsburg with some 3000, and at Paw-paw tunnel in Morgan with some 12,000 or 15,000. I think it very uncertain whether an advance upon Winchester is intended at this time. Their purpose in crossing the river is probably to rebuild the railroad. When this is done we shall probably be attacked here. If the force of the enemy is far superior to our own, — and it probably will be, I think, — we shall retire from the place without making a defence. So don't be alarmed at any rumors you may hear.

Since my return we have had a very idle time. My duty is to take charge of the regiment in the absence of the Colonel, and as he is here I have nothing at all to do. I am very anxious to get a job of some sort which will give me occupation.

The wish which lies nearest my heart is for your comfort and happiness in my absence. I will write regularly so that you will get my letters on Sunday morning when you go to church. As soon as you hear what was the fate of Brother's two boys at Fort Donelson, write me about it.

Love, Frank

Activity around the enemy position indicated a general advance by General N. P. Banks. On March 11th., Jackson, noting this, began moving his troops to Strasburg, eighteen miles from Winchester. On March 7th. and again on the 11th. the men were prepared to meet the Union General. Ashby's scouting forays and Jackson's readiness convinced Banks that his adversary was too well prepared.[1]

Strasburg, March 13, 1862

I doubt not you have heard of many bloody battles, actual and anticipated, about Winchester for the last few days, and, if you credited every flying rumor, have been somewhat apprehensive of my safety. You will then, I doubt not, be surprised to hear that we have had no fight; none killed except perhaps one or two of our cavalry pickets; none captured except some thirty or forty who stayed behind in Winchester, many of them, I doubt not, wishing to be taken. Twice since my last letter we have had every reason to expect an

_____
[1]Henderson, p. 173.

engagement. Last Friday evening the long roll, always a signal for battle, was sounded and the regiment formed under arms. We marched out and took our position and remained there for a day, but the enemy did not come up. On Tuesday evening the long roll was beaten again, and we took our position, the enemy having advanced his whole force within two or three miles of us. We remained there until dark, but were not attacked. Then we moved back five miles on the pike, and yesterday morning came to this place. Here we are, and what next? Will we continue our retreat or fight? No one knows. Jackson always shows fight, and hence we never know what he means. Don't suffer yourself to be alarmed by any rumors which you read or hear. So soon as we have an engagement, if I get out of it, I will write to you, enclosing the letter to your father, requesting him to send it out immediately. So soon as we have an engagement, everybody will be writing letters, and, I doubt not, your father will send you immediately any reliable news that may come.

The militia, I see from the papers, are called out, and John Fitzgerald will have to go. Give him the shotgun to take with him. I don't know what you ought to do to supply his place. Consult with your father, and do what you think best. You can leave the place and go to town if you don't feel safe there. Your happiness, Love, I value and wish to secure above everything else.

Love, Frank

On a windy day on March 15th., Jackson, in trying to draw Banks up the valley, dispatched his men from Strasburg to Mount Jackson, a distance of twenty four miles. Banks, noting this, sent General James Shields to intercept Jackson and the Union General entered Strasburg on the 19th.[2]

Mount Jackson, March 19, 1862

We left our encampment near Strasburg last Saturday, and reached this place on Monday, where appearances indicate that we are settled in peace and quiet for a while. There is some skirmishing between our pickets and those of the enemy about twenty miles from here, but I believe the enemy have not left Winchester in any force, and, I imagine, will not until the roads and weather will admit of an advance on the other side of the mountain on Johnston.

The time passes very dull with me, as I have nothing to do, the Colonel and Lieut. Col. of the regiment both being here and doing what little there is to be done. Some days ago I met with your sister Martha, who had come down to the camp to see Mr. Williamson. She was much alarmed at the expected approach of the enemy, and in doubt what to do. My advice to her was to remain at home if they came, letting everything go on as usual. They would take such of her property as they needed, but, I believed, would do no further injury. Their policy, so far as I can learn, has been, in Winchester and the counties which they occupy, to conciliate the people. I doubt not it will be their principle everywhere. I am glad they indicate their purpose to carry on the war on the principles of civilized warfare, as it

---

[2]Ibid., p. 175.

exempts the women and children left at home by our soldiers from the savage barbarities of their vengeance. If the fate of war brings my own home within their lines, it will be some consolation to know that you, my dearling wife, and our dear little children are not subjected to insult and injury at the hands of the invaders. Whilst their occupancy may deprive me of the fond letters of a loving wife, giving the glad news that all are well at home, which is now my greatest source of happiness, I shall be comforted by the hope and belief that they are left to enjoy uninterrupted the necessary comforts of life. Whilst it is a sad thought to give up one's home to the enemy, with many of us it is destined to be a necessity which will contribute more than all other causes to the ultimate achievement of our independence. It is utterly impossible to defend every section.

Just here, Love, I will change the subject to say that, whilst writing, I have received your letter of the 15th. inst. We may never meet again, as you say, Love. We know nothing of the future, but I trust the day of our final separation is far distant. The obituaries which I find in the paper from home remind me that those who remain at home, as well as those who have joined the army, die. Of the thousand who have left our county for the army, I suppose not more than fifty have died from disease or in battle. Nearly as large a proportion of those at home I expect have died. Life is uncertain everywhere, Love, and you should not infer from my being in the army that you and I may not see much of life together yet. I am glad I can't turn aside the dark veil which covers the future and look at the good and evil in store for me.

I am sorry that Galla had the luck to break the likeness, but glad that I have a place in the dear little fellow's memory and that he wanted to see his papa. I am glad, too, to learn that you have found in little Mary Fitzgerald a post-office messenger, and that you can get the papers and my letters without sending one of the hands and stopping work on the farm for the purpose. I have heretofore written so that my letters would reach you on Sunday when you went to church, but now I can write at any time. I felt gratified to learn that Fitz was exempt from the militia draft, although it was selfish and unpatriotic, as he would make a good soldier. I am very anxious that you should be comfortable and contented at home; and as he is so faithful and industrious, I am sure he will be of great service to you, and that you will feel much safer from his being there.

And now, Love, as I have some matters requiring my attention this evening, I will bid you good-bye and bring my letter to a close. Give a kiss to the dear little boys for me, and for yourself accept my best love.

Love, Frank

CHAPTER IX

THE CADETS WERE
BEHIND OUR BRIGADE

Information was received by Jackson from intelligence that the Union General N. P. Banks was moving his army from Winchester with the intention of joining McClellan. This prompted the Confederate General to attempt an interception of Banks before the Union troops could join forces.

On the twenty third of March Jackson directed his troops to move on Kernstown, a spot four miles south of Winchester which was reached by two o'clock Sunday afternoon. Col. Turner Ashby reported to Jackson that he believed the enemy in a rear guard action possessed less than three thousand men. To Jackson's chagrin the force proved to be twice this strength under General James Shield's command.[1]

Kernstown was turned into a bloody battle field and the fighting lasted until sundown when General Richard G. Garnett leading the Stonewall Brigade ordered a hasty retreat. For this action on April 1st. he was placed under arrest by Jackson and relieved of his command. The battle cost Jackson seven hundred casualties.[2]

Shields took pride in knowing that he was the only Union General that ever whipped Stonewall Jackson in battle.[3]

The main body of Jackson's men moved to a wooded area the next day at Newtown about four and a half miles from the battlefield where they set up a bivouac.[4]

Mount Jackson, Wednesday, March 26, 1862

The robins on the trees around me sing merrily this morning, as if this part of the world was enjoying its usual calm, and the soldiers are laughing and talking as cheerfully as if apprehension of danger and alarm for the future was the last of their thoughts. Since last Thursday, when we started towards Winchester, we have had exciting times. We were engaged on Sunday in a fiercer struggle, more obstinately maintained on our side, than that at Manassas last July. The battle between the infantry, the artillery having been engaged in firing some time before, commenced about five o'clock and ended about six o'clock, when our lines gave way and retreated in disorder

[1]Douglas, p. 45.
[2]Dabney, p. 546.
[3]Douglas, p. 46.
[4]Vandiver, p. 207.

to our wagons, about four miles from the battlefield. Our loss in killed, wounded, and missing, I suppose, may reach 400. Col. Echols had his arm broken. The next morning after the battle we left in good order about ten o'clock, and came some seven miles in this direction, where we encamped and cooked dinner. Before we left the enemy appeared with their cannon, and as we were leaving commenced firing upon us. One of their shells burst in our regiment, killing four and wounding several more. We came that night — Monday — to Woodstock, and on yesterday came here, some ten miles farther. We keep some artillery and cavalry in our rear, close to the lines of the enemy, who check his advance and keep us advised of what is going on. We remain on our encampment with wagons packed and everything in order to move until the afternoon, when we move back. To you this would seem exciting, yet the soldiers sit around in squads, laughing and talking as if they enjoyed the sport. I think it likely, if the enemy advances, we will retreat up towards Staunton. His force which we engaged at Winchester was some 15,000, according to the best estimate we can get of it, whilst ours did not exceed 4000. I think we will not venture on a battle against such odds, but will wait for reinforcements and continue to retire if we are pressed. You may be certain to hear from me if I get out safe from another engagement.

Love, Frank

On April 1st. General Charles S. Winder was placed in command of the Stonewall Brigade.[5]

Bivouac near Woodstock, April 1, 1862

Last Thursday I received an order from Gen. Jackson to take charge of four companies and report to Col. Ashby for duty on the advance-guard. I go down occasionally to take a view of the enemy's pickets, but most of the time have been lying idle. The enemy are encamped around Strasburg and for some four miles this side, where they seem disposed to remain quiet for the present. The whole country bears the appearance of a funeral, everything is so quiet. In a ride yesterday along our lines, I scarcely saw any person moving about, and all work on the farms seemed suspended; many of the houses seemed to be deserted. The soldiers alone seem to exhibit the appearance of contentment and happiness. A mode of life which once seemed so strange and unnatural habit has made familiar to us, and if peace ever comes many of them will be disqualified for a life of industry.

I have seen, in a Baltimore paper, a list of the prisoners taken from the battle at Winchester. It is very gratifying to find that some are captured whose fate was involved in doubt. Among them I am pleased to find the name of Charley Rollins, whom I saw upon the field behaving very gallantly. Send word to his mother if you have an opportunity. Capt. Morrison and Lieut. Lyle of the College Co. are on the list. Two captains and one Lieut. were captured from our regiment. Our loss in killed and wounded and captured, I expect, will reach 500. I do not think we had over 2500 men engaged, whilst the enemy probably had four times the number, consisting, for the most

[5]Vandiver, P. 212.

part, of troops which have been in service for the last year under [William S.] Rosecrans in Western Virginia, than whom they have no better troops in the field. I never expect to see troops fight better than ours did. Our force is rapidly increasing from the militia who are coming in and will be used in filling up the volunteer companies. Many of those sick and absent on furlough are returning, and with all, I think, we will have a force sufficient to meet the enemy with success. Until our force is increased and reorganized, I think we shall continue to retreat with-out another battle.

Love, Frank

Banks and Jackson faced each other for two weeks while each awaited a move from the other. After a time the Federal troops began threatening an advance toward Mount Jackson resulting in Jackson's decision to move southward toward Rude's Hill and the New Market area.[6]

The situation was critical because Banks seized New Market and threatened to occupy Swift Run Gap thereby cutting communications between Jackson and General Joe Johnston. To keep this pass open, Jackson ordered a forced march by his men. On the 19th. Jackson crossed the Shenandoah at Conrad's store where they moved to the foot of Swift Run Gap.[7]

Jackson was intent on destroying Bank's force. To do this the Confederate General intended to draw Bank's units into Swift Run Gap where the Federal forces would be cut off.[8]

Since Banks seemed to be content to stay at Harrisonburg, Jackson decided to attack General R. H. Milroy who was deployed around Staunton.[9]

During the 29th of April Ashby and his men with the aid of an artillery barrage attempted to rout Banks forward position which pressure continued throughout the next day. The same day Jackson began marching southward toward Port Republic and as the men marched the weather turned bad. Along the east side of the Shenandoah they trudged for sixteen miles and men were falling out due to cold throughout the march. Upon reaching the village, Jackson decided to bivouac his men at Brown's gap.[10]

On the fourth of May, Jackson's advanced guard arriving at Staunton was joined by a detachment of two hundred V. M. I. cadets commanded by General F. H. Smith. The nest day the rest of the men reached the town at which time Jackson ordered a halt to determine where the enemy was and to replenish his supplies.[11]

---

[6]Chambers, Vol. I, p. 472.
[7]Henderson, p. 208-9.
[8]Ibid., p. 213.
[9]Ibid., p. 221.
[10]Henderson, p. 216-7.
[11]Chambers, Vol. I, p. 502.

Jackson's men met the Federals under the command of General R. H. Milroy and Robert C. Schenk on May 8th. at the town of McDowell. Concerning the battle Jackson sent the following dispatch, "God blessed our arms with victory at McDowell yesterday."[12] It was a victory but the fruits of gain were costly. Jackson's men sustained four hundred ninety eight casualties while the enemy sustained two hundred fifty six. One of the severest loss' in wounded to the Confederates was Brigadier General Edward Johnson who had immediate command during the hottest part of the fighting.[13]

McDowell, May 9, 1862

Before this reaches you, you will have heard alarming rumors of the fight on yesterday, and feel, I know, much anxiety for my safety. I was not hurt, for the reason that I was not in the fight. No part of our brigade was engaged, the enemy being whipped off the field before it came. But little, if any, more than one-third of our forces were engaged. The fight began late in the evening in an unexpected attack from the enemy, and lasted about an hour. Our loss, I expect, will reach 60 killed and 300 wounded. They began their retreat early this morning in the direction of Pendleton County. We pursued them to-day some twelve or fifteen miles, capturing six or seven persons. They left considerable quantity of tents and provisions, but burned most of them. I am indebted to this source for the sheet upon which I write.

Well, you want to know when we are going to have another fight? There is no telling, but I think to-morrow we shall take the end of the road which leads to Harrisonburg. I saw Matthew after the fight was over, and he, like myself, I suppose had not been in it. The cadets were behind our brigade, and, though I have not seen White Williamson, he is, I doubt not, unhurt except by the hard march. The company from Brownsburg, formerly Carey's, suffered very severely, the captain, Whitmore, being killed and one of the lieutenants severely wounded.

I left Staunton the day I wrote you last week and joined the army at Port Republic. Since then we have been marching every day but one which we spent in Staunton. And now, darling, I will bid you good-bye.

Love, Frank

*   *   *   *   *   *

Friday, May 16, 1862

I don't know where to date my letter. We left Highland yesterday, and are now on the road to Harrisonburg, seven or eight miles from the Augusta line. We have had three days' rain, and still a cloudy sky threatening more rain. The road is now very bad, and as every wagon which passes makes it deeper, it will soon be impassable. The weather

---

[12]*Battles and Leaders of the Civil War* Grant-Lee edition, Vol. II, p. 287, 4 Volumes, New York, 1939. (Hereafter cited as B & L).

[13]Chambers, Vol. I, p. 505.

is worse upon us than last winter. Then the ground was frozen and we had the satisfaction at least of being dry — having dry clothes and dry blankets. But now everything is wet and we have no tents. It has had no happy effect upon my health. Yesterday I left the brigade to stay in a house a few days, but think I shall join it again to-morrow.

We had constant expectation of a fight while we were in Pendleton. We supposed Jackson would certainly make the attack on the morning after we reached Franklin, and every one was surprised when we turned to march in this direction. No one ever knows where he is going or what his plans are. I suppose his destination now is the Valley, where he will consolidate with Ewell and move towards Winchester. But at present, I think, he will be disposed to give his troops a week's rest. They need it badly, as they have been marching for nearly three weeks since they left their last encampment.

We have not yet had an election in our regiment for field officers, and I feel more unsettled than ever before. I am not sure that I will be elected, and not sure that I will not. If I were elected by a mere majority, and knew that I did not have the good-will of a large portion of my regiment, I am not sure that I would want the place. I have been absent from the regiment on detached service of one kind and another, and when with them I have always been disposed to be rather rigid. The two causes combined have not given me a strong hold upon their affections. So you see I am rather perplexed with doubts — don't know which end of the road to take, if either. Whatever be the result, I trust I shall do nothing to forfeit the good opinion of my friends; and if I return home, it will be for reasons which now and hereafter shall meet the approval of my judgement. I wish heartily the election was over and I knew my destiny.

Love, Frank

On June 6th. Turner Ashby was shot and breathed his last in the arms of Lt. Jim Thompson. Frank Paxton had lost a dear friend.[14]

The election that Frank had mentioned in his last letter was soon after this held under what was known as the "Disorganization Act" of the Confederate Congress, and Major Paxton, with many other officers whose strict discipline was not relished by men, failed to be reelected. He was thus relieved from any further obligation to continue in the service, but his heart was too much in the cause to permit him to abandon the army at such a time. He accepted a place on the staff of his old commander, General Jackson, as a volunteer aide without pay, and in this capacity took part in the seven days' fight before Richmond. After a brief visit to his home, on July 22, 1862, he returned to the army to resume his position as volunteer aide.

[14]Douglas, p. 86.

CHAPTER X

THE ONLY OBJECTION TO MY POSITION IS THAT I DRAW NO PAY

The Stonewall brigade was fast becoming the most famous organization in the Confederacy. For about two months they had been in constant battle. After leaving Elk Run on April 29th. up until they fell back on Richmond on July 8th. they had never stayed for more than 4 days at one site. Jackson began trying to convince members of Congress that 'McClellan's army was manifestly beaten, incapable of moving until it had been reorganized and reinforced. There was danger,' he foretold, 'that the fruits of victory would be lost, as they had been lost after Manassas. The Confederates should leave Richmond and carry the horrors of invasion across the border. 'This was the only way,' he said, 'to bring the war to an end.'[1]

Camp near Gordonsville, July 23, 1862

I reached here on yesterday, and now hold the place which I had when I left — volunteer aide to Gen. Jackson. The position is very agreeable, and the only objection to it is that I draw no pay and pay my own expenses. I feel quite at home, and am entirely satisfied to spend the rest of the war in this position. Everything here seems so quiet. The troops are drilling, and there is every indication that the troops will rest here for some time. Considering the severe hardships through which they have passed since the war began, it is very much needed. Everything has a happy, quiet appearance, such as I have not seen in the army since we were in camp this time last year after the battle of Manassas.

I am sorry to have left you with so much work on hand, but hope you may bear it patiently. There is more need now than ever that as much should be made from the farm as possible, as I am drawing no pay. And now, darling, good-bye. I will write you frequently and let you know how I am getting along. I hope you will be as contented and happy as possible, and manage matters just as you please, and I will be satisfied.

Love, Frank

*　　*　　*　　*　　*　　*

August 3, 1862

For some days I have been expecting that every mail would bring me a letter from home, but have been disappointed. I am sure a letter is on the way, and that you would not suffer two weeks to pass

---

[1] Henderson, p. 397-8.

without writing to me. I wrote to you some ten days ago, just after I got here. It may be this did not reach you, and you do not know where I am. I am getting to feel used to the army and to the idea of staying in it until I see the end of the war, or it sees the end of me. The work entrusted to me is highly honorable and very agreeable. I think it will be sufficient to keep me employed and make me as happy as I have ever been in the service. The only objection to it is that my labor is gratuitous and I draw no pay. I shall try and make my expense account as small as possible. The army is more quiet than I have ever known it. The enemy have considerable force some thirty or forty miles from us, amounting possibly to 30,000 men. Their cavalry and ours are occasionally skirmishing, and yesterday had quite a severe engagement with one of our regiments at Orange C. H. [Court House]. They are said to have had some three regiments against our one, and, so far as I can learn, we got the worst of it. No very serious damage, however, as our killed and wounded are only fifteen.

To-day — Sunday — is very quiet, and reminds me much of a Sunday at home, the usual work being suspended. Formerly everything went on as usual on any day, but now the drills and ordinary work of the week are suspended on Sunday. Whilst employment here will make me contented, for there is no use in grieving about what must be bourne, yet I heartily wish that I was home with you and our dear little children. Affection and sympathy attract me towards home as the dearest place on earth, but duty to my country and respect for my own manhood require that I should forego this happiness until the war ends — as end it must, sooner or later. I trust, darling, that you will be as contented and happy as you can under the circumstances. The inconveniences to which you are subjected are just the same which all other ladies have to bear. You, at least, have all the comforts of home and necessaries of life, whilst the wife and little ones of many gallant men in the service are exiles from their homes or without the necessaries of life. It is a poor consolation for your own troubles that others are worse; but it is alike the dictate of piety and virtue to bear them in patience, and thus show that you merit a better fate. The war must end some day. We may never live to see it. But we owe to ourselves to cherish the hope that we may one day live happily together again, and there will be bright sunshine after the storm which now envelops us.

Love, Frank

In mid-August, 1862, the Federal General John Pope headed toward Gordonsville accompanied by Bank's and Franz Sigel's Corps for the purpose of cutting the Confederate route from Richmond to Shenandoah. At the same time, Irwin McDowell was entraining at Washington to meet them at Gordonsville.

Jackson crossed the Rapidan River and Banks with two divisions was ordered to hold the Confederates at Cedar Mountain while Pope's main force cut behind them. The orders unknowingly, were changed from "hold," to "attack," and as the Union General proceeded to carry out his orders his 3500 men were swamped by 20,000 Jackson men.[2]

[2]Fletcher, Pratt, *A Short History of the Civil War*, p. 140, Pocket Books, Cardinal Edition, New York, 1952.

Jackson declared the battle at Cedar Mountain a victory and the booty consisted of 400 prisoners, one gun, three colors, and 5302 small arms. As for casualties his dead numbered 220 and wounded 1047.[3]

During the 27th., 28th., and 29th. of August Jackson's troops were engaged in one of their costliest battles of the war — The Second Battle of Manassas. The Stonewall Brigade was reduced to regimental strength when 200 of its men were killed or wounded.[4]

Paxton told Jackson, "General, the victory has been won by the determined valor of our soldiers, by plain hard fighting."

Jackson answered him quietly, "Don't forget it has been won by the help of God."[5]

—GENERALS IN GREY
GEN. W. B. TALIAFERRO

—BATTLES & LEADERS
GEN. TURNER ASHBY

—GENERALS IN GRAY
GEN. R. B. GARNETT

—GENERALS IN GREY
GEN. C. S. WINDER

[3]O.R., Vol. XII, p. 180.
[4]O.R., Vol. XII, p. 661, 663, 663-4.
[5]Douglas, p. 143.

CHAPTER XI

IN ONE MINUTE
FIVE HUNDRED MEN DIED

On Sunday August 31st. the rains came and everyone was drenched. It was difficult to bury the dead, care for the wounded, and collect arms and ammunition; in addition the Union soldiers were strongly encamped at Centerville.[1]

The next day Jackson marched past Chantilly, an old southern mansion, which had been partly destroyed by the enemy. Sadly noting the destruction which had been caused, the men moved slowly toward Fairfax Courthouse. A short skirmish ensued at Ox Hill near Germantown which at times was softer than the thunder. The Union army lost two able soldiers when General's Phil Kearny and I. I. Stevens were mortally wounded.[2]

> Fairfax C. H., Sept. 1, 1862
>
> My darling Wife: I have only time to say that we were fighting on Wednesday, Thursday, Friday, and Saturday, and I am well. The last was a very severe battle and in large force. The enemy was badly routed. His force consisted of McClellan and Pope unified.
>
> Ever Yours, Frank

The report of General Jackson of these battles makes mention of Paxton, "In the prompt transmission of orders (Cedar Mountain) great assistance was received from Maj. E. F. Paxton, Acting Asst. Adj. General. Desiring to avoid delay, I directed my Acting Asst. Adj. Genl. to order Jackson's Division forward." and "In the transmission of orders (2nd. Manassas) I was greatly assisted during expedition by the following members of my staff; Col. A. Smart, Asst. Inspector General, Major E. F. Paxton, Acting Assistant Adjutant General."[3]

Clamor in the south called for an invasion of Maryland which coincided with General Lee's appraisal of the military situation. The Army of Northern Virginia marched toward the Potomac.[4]

On September 3rd. during the march, Jackson ordered General A. P. Hill's leading brigade to halt. Hill stormed to the head of the

---

[1] Douglas, p. 144.
[2] Henderson, p. 480-1.
[3] O.R., Vol. XII, part II, p. 185.
[4] Douglas Southall Freeman, *Lee's Lieutenants*, Vol. I, p. 144-5, New York, 1942-4. (Hereafter cited as Freeman).

column and demanded of General [Edward L.] Thomas who was leading the column the reason for the stop.

"I halted because General Jackson ordered me to," replied Thomas.

Hill galloped to Jackson's position and hastily drew his sword and offered it to the General with the comment, "If you take command of my troops in my presence, take my sword also."

Jackson returned, "Put your sword up and consider yourself under arrest."[5]

Upon reaching Frederick, Maryland, Hill formerly requested a copy of the charges against him and acting Assistant General Major Paxton told him, "Should the interests of the services require your case be brought up before a courts martial a copy of the charges and specifications will be furnished in accordance with army regulations." and continuing the directive from Jackson, Paxton said, "In the meantime you will remain with your division."[6]

The Generals in camp drew the attention of the people in the little Maryland town. Lee and Jackson feeling ill stayed close to their tents during the morning and wouldn't talk to the populace. Jackson did not go to church on that morning but in the evening he asked Joseph Morrison and Kyd Douglas to accompany him to a worship service and Major Paxton issued the following pass.[7]

Hdqs. Valley District
September 7, 1862

Guards and Pickets:
　　Pass Major General T. J. Jackson and two staff officers and attendant to Frederick to church, to return tonight.

By Command of Maj. Genl. Jackson
E. F. Paxton
A. A. Gen'l

The party attended the German reformed church where in his sermon, Dr. Zacharias gave a prayer for the President of The United States. The Doctor later was said to have had a great deal of courage in praying for the President of the United States in the presence of Stonewall. The pastor failed to realize that Jackson was asleep during the prayer.[8]

Frederick, Maryland, Sunday, September 7, 1862
　　Your two last letters came to hand yesterday, and I was indeed very happy to hear from you. The date of my letter will surprise you.

[5]*The Judiah Hotchkiss Collection*, Box 8, in the Library of Congress, Manuscript Division.
[6]Chambers, Vol. II, p. 181.
[7]Douglas, p. 150.
[8]Ibid., p. 151.

You would have thought it hardly possible that the fortunes of war should have turned in our favor that this quiet Sabbath would find use here quietly encamped beyond the limits of our own Confederacy. It has cost us much of our best blood and much hardship, but it is a magnificent result, which, I trust will secure our recognition in Europe, and be a stem at least toward peace with our enemies. We left the Rappahannock two weeks ago to-morrow, and such a week as the first was has no parallel in the war. Two days' severe march brought us about fifty miles to Manassas. That night we had an engagement with the enemy, in which the place was captured and some prisoners. [sic] The next day there was another battle, in which Mr. Newman was wounded. That night — Wednesday — we evacuated the place and took up our position adjoining the old battle ground, and that evening we had another severe engagement, in which Maj.-Gen. [Richard] Ewell was severely wounded and our loss very heavy. The next day — Friday — we were attacked by the enemy in much larger forces, but we repulsed the enemy and at night both armies occupied about the same ground. We expected the battle to be renewed the next morning. The enemy had time to collect his whole force, Pope and McClellan combined, and we had brought up all we had on this side of the Rappahannock. For a while, the lines were unusually quiet, but after a while the picket-firing began to increase, and soon the whole line was engaged. The assault upon our line was very severe, and for a while the tide of battle seemed to turn against us; but our men stubbornly resisted the assault, and soon the enemy's line gave way, flying in confusion, our artillery playing upon them as they retreated. Our lines were then pushed forward, and by night the enemy was driven from every position. It was a splendid victory, partly fought on the same ground with the battle of Manassas last year. We sustained a very heavy loss, but how much I have no idea. The next day we moved towards Fairfax C. H. The next day — Monday — we had another severe engagement. Tuesday we spent at rest and in cooking. Wednesday we started in this direction, and reached here early on yesterday, without meeting any further obstructions. What next — where do we go — and what is to be done? We will probably know by the end of next week what our General means to do with us. I think it likely we will not stay here, and that this time next week will find us either in Pennsylvania or Baltimore.

I heartily wish with you that the war was over and we were all at home again. But our success depends upon the pertinacity with which we stick to the fight. I think it may not last through another winter. I spend but little time now thinking about business on the farm. I trust it all to you. My duties here are numerous and responsible, occupying my time and mind so completely that I have but little opportunity to think of much else. Not enough, however, to keep me from thinking of dear wife and little ones left at home, and fondly hoping that the day may soon come when I will be with them. It may never come. My fate may be that of many others. Whatever the future may have in store for me, I trust that I am prepared to meet it with becoming resignation.

And now, darling, I will take leave of you. Think of me often, and believe me, with much love, ever yours.

Frank

On September 8th. General Lee spoke to the people of Maryland saying, "No restraint upon your free will is intended. No intimidation will be allowed. This army will respect your choice whatever it may be; and while the Southern people will rejoice to welcome you to your natural position among them, they will only welcome you when you come of your free will."[9]

Jackson moved early on September 10th. traveling through Frederick by sunrise then into Turner's gap and reaching Boonsboro at nightfall where they spent the night.[10]

September the 11th. found Jackson crossing the Potomac at Williamsport while the band played, "Carry Me Back to Ole Virginy to the Virginy Shore."[11] That evening the troops moved toward Martinsburg camping about four miles from the village. When Jackson and his men entered the town the next morning the townspeople gave them a cheering reception.[12]

Col. Dixon S. Miles, Federal commander at Harper's Ferry was informed on the 13th. that Jackson was approaching. He nervously awaited the Confederates attack while apprehensively hoping for reinforcement before Jackson arrived. That evening Jackson encamped at Halltown, two miles above Harper's Ferry at Bolivar Heights.[13]

Lost Order, S.O. 191, addressed to Major General D. H. Hill was found on September the 14th. by private B. W. Mitchell of the 27th. Indiana Infantry. This gave disposition of Lee's troops in the area.[14]

General James A. Walker and General Lafayette McLaws were supposed to occupy Loudoun Heights and begin bombarding Harper's Ferry early on the 13th. Jackson seeing no sign of them summoned his signal officer, Captain Joseph L. Bartlett to try to contact the heights. Bartlett and his men failed to receive any signal until long after darkness when a courier reported that Walker was in position.[15] Refer to Appendix for the message sent during the battle.

At 3:00 A.M. on the 15th. [Major Kyd] Douglas was dispatched by Jackson to direct General D. R. Jones to move his skirmishers forward at daylight toward Bolivar Heights which was controlled by the enemy. Confederate artillery began laying down a barrage at daylight and the line of attack showed Hill on the right, Ewell covering the center and Jackson's old division on the

---

[9]Ibid.
[10]Henderson, p. 503.
[11]Douglas, p. 155.
[12]Ibid., p. 156.
[13]Ibid., p. 158.
[14]Freeman, Vol. II, p. 173.
[15]Vandiver, p. 385.

left. The battle continued until a white flag rose above Harper's Ferry. The Union General Julius White asked for surrender terms from Jackson and was told that the surrender would have to be unconditional. The Union General agreed and was turned over to General A. P. Hill by Jackson.[16]

Surrender cost the Federals 12,500 prisoners, 13,000 arms, 73 pieces of artillery, and approximately two hundred wagons together with their provisions.[17]

General Jackson with a portion of his staff rode toward Harper's Ferry on the 15th. and noticed Union soldiers on both sides of the road peering at him. Some saluted and one exclaimed, "Boys he's not much for looks, but if we'd had him we wouldn't have been caught in this trap."[18]

Lee decided to concentrate his troops around Sharpsburg and Jackson's men in a severe two day march reached an area in the vicinity of the town. Had McClellan attacked prior to Jackson's arrival the Confederates would have been badly outnumbered. With the arrival of Jackson the sides were relatively balanced.[19]

The battle of Sharpsburg was fought on the 17th. of September and proved to be one of the bitterest and costliest struggles of the war. Known in the north as Antietam, it lasted twelve hours and cost the Confederates 9500 casualties as compared to the Union's 12,000. A summary in the *Charleston Courier* stated that, "They [Confederates] fought until they were cut to pieces, and then retreated only because they had fired their last round!"[20]

—BATTLES & LEADERS

Jackson's foot cavalry on the march against Pope.

---

[16]Douglas, p. 160, 161.
[17]O.R., Pt. 1, pp. 951, 960 & 961.
[18]Douglas, p. 162.
[19]Freeman, p. 201, 202.
[20]Chambers, Vol. II, p. 224.

CHAPTER XII

OUR VICTORIES
SEEM TO SETTLE NOTHING

On the 22nd. of September Abraham Lincoln signed the Emancipation Proclamation.

September 23rd. General Jackson recommended that Paxton be appointed Brigadier General because in Jackson's words, "There is no officer under the grade proposed whom I can recommend with such confidence." Several officers resented this and one resigned. The promotion was officially delivered on November 6th. and Paxton took over the Stonewall Brigade. (See Appendix)

General J. R. Jones stated in an official report that stragglers were congesting the area and he wanted the reaction of Paxton. (See Appendix)

While in camp at Martinsburg a gentleman of the countryside asked General Jackson and some of his aides to eat supper with him. Before serving he asked whether the officers wanted their appetizers straight or with water.

"Have you any white sugar?" asked Jackson.

The man obliged the General and Jackson announced, "Come gentlemen, let's take a drink."

Major Paxton stated that he did not drink and Kyd Douglas declined due to ill health. After the appetizers were consumed supper was served and the home cooked meal looked mighty good to soldiers who were used to army rations.[1]

Lee presented to President Davis on the 2nd. of October a reorganization plan whereby the Army of Northern Virginia would consist of two corps commanded by Longstreet and Jackson.[2]

Bunker Hill, Va., October 5, 1862

The army was never so quiet as now, the general impression prevailing that we contemplate no advance upon the enemy and that he contemplates none upon us. We are lying quiet to gather in our absentees and recover from the losses which we have sustained in the active work of the last sixty days. When this is accomplished winter will probably have set in, and the work of this year closed. I fear our troops are to suffer much from want of clothing, and that our

[1]Douglas, p. 182.
[2]Chambers, Vol. II, p. 236.

supplies will prove greatly inadequate for our wants.

Whilst the army has been apparently idle, I have been unusually busy during the last week. Everybody seems to be making application for something, and my office is crowded with business. I do scarcely any writing, leaving it all to my clerk, Mr. Figgat. If I undertook to do the writing, my eyes would not last long. But as it is, I think I shall be able to do my work without injury. My office is one of much importance and responsibility, and I trust I may be able to fill it without suffering injury to my sight. I think, Love, if this war lasts much longer, you will get to be a pretty good farmer. It really seems as if it would last forever. Both parties getting used to it, and the signs of peace and quiet are less, if anything, now than this time last year.

I heartily wish I were at home with you and our dear little boys. It is the wish of many thousands of my comrades who have left loved wives and children at home to mourn their absence and grieve over the danger and hardships to which they are exposed. God grant that we may all soon be gratified — that the fervent prayer for our return may soon be answered. When we do, I think it will be with a more grateful appreciation of the blessings which we were accustomed every day to enjoy.

Now, darling, I will bid you good-bye. Think of me often and cherish the fond love which has marked our intercourse thus far through life as our greatest source of happiness.

Love, Frank

*　*　*　*　*　*

Bunker Hill, Va., October 12, 1862

It has not been three months since I left home. I can hardly realize that it has been so long, the time has passed so rapidly. During this period I have had the pleasure of participating in what history will record as the most astonishing expeditions of war, for the severity of the battles fought and the hardships endured by our soldiers. And now it seems like settling down to idleness. The last week was one of quiet and stagnation like the week before. I have not been in a saddle now for two weeks, and have not been half a mile from my camp since we came to our present encampment. Yet I have been kept so busy that the time passed fast enough. I have had general charge of the orders and correspondence, which has given me full employment. We may have some more activity this fall, but I am inclined to think the campaign is over. It is too late now for either side to think of accomplishing much before the winter sets in. Our army is in splendid condition. It has been rapidly increasing during the last three weeks by conscripts and convalescents who have been coming in. If the enemy cross the Potomac to begin the offensive, we shall, I think, have another great battle near this place, and I feel sure that it will be a splendid victory for us. Our victories, though, seem to settle nothing; to bring us no nearer the end of the war. It is only so many killed and wounded, leaving the work of blood to go on with renewed vigor. Like everything else, it must have an end sooner or later.

And now, darling, I will take leave of you, hoping you may have a good time getting through with your complicated troubles on the farm. No doubt you think I devote little of my time to thinking about them. True, because of my work here occupies my whole time except

Sunday, when, by Gen. Lee's order, we are to remain idle unless necessity compels the work. Kiss our dear little boys for me, and remind them of their absent papa. How I wish I could see you all for a little while! But I must not think of it until Christmas.

Love, Frank

While at Bunker Hill, working parties were dispatched by Jackson to destroy the Baltimore & Ohio railroad tracks between Hedgesville and Halltown. Confederate details set fire to railway ties causing the rails to warp and leaving the track useless for the Federals. The demolition squads then destroyed tanks, culverts, bridges, and telegraph lines causing a serious rupture in enemy communications.[3]

Martinsburg, October 19, 1862

I have spent a busy Sunday, superintending the destruction of the railroad here, and will spend what little remains of the day in writing you a short note. It is a bad chance for a letter, as I write on my pocket-book resting on my knee. I received your letter of the 9th. ult., and was glad to hear from you. I felt to-day as though I were at my old trade — destroying the railroad — which I was at eighteen months ago. Last week we thought there was a chance for another battle, as it was reported the enemy was advancing. But it turned out to be only a scouting party. With that exception, we have had a very quiet time.

Love, Frank

Important persons were visiting Jackson's position and one was Colonel Garnet Wolsely of the British army who later became its commander in chief. Also from Britain were two newsmen from the *London Illustrated News*.[4]

Jackson, deciding to move closer to the Shenandoah River, marched to Charlestown where he encamped for several days then on to Millwood where a permanent camp was prepared.[5]

Camp near Charlestown, October 25, 1862

This is a dreary, rainy Sunday; every one idle and at a loss for employment. We came down on yesterday to tear up the railroad; the job is about finished, I think, and we would leave now but for the rain. We will return to Bunker Hill, I suppose, to-morrow. It really seems as if the winter would come before we had any further active work. I care but little whether we have any or not, and feel ready for it, whatever it may be. Some indulge hope that it will be over this winter. I do not know. Our duty is to prepare for a most vigorous prosecution of the war next spring, and be prepared for the worst that may come. We are in the hands of a just God, who will give us peace

[3]Chambers, Vol. II, p. 249 and Douglas, p. 183.
[4]Douglas, p. 186.
[5]Ibid., p. 195.

when we deserve it. I heartily wish, Love, that I was at home with you. No honor or promotion could tempt me to stay here if my duty and self-respect did not make it imperative. My manhood is involved in a faithful and fearless sticking to the job until it is finished, or it finishes me, as it has done many good men. With such a future before me, dark and uncertain enough, I am sure, I try to do whatever is required of me well and cheerfully. I have much reason to be gratified at the many evidences of good opinion which I have received from Gen'l. Jackson and all under whom I have served. I trust I may be able to get a short furlough to visit home this winter, and I look forward to it with much pleasure. The first freezing, snowy weather we have to stop all active work, I shall make an effort to spend a few weeks with you.

Love, Frank

—BATTLES & LEADERS
Jackson's men defending the railroad cut at 2nd Manassas.

CHAPTER XIII

P.S. I HAVE RECEIVED AN ORDER CONFERRING UPON ME THE TITLE OF BRIGADIER-GENERAL

By the 26th of October, McClellan decided to move. His main thrust at Berlin was noted by Lee and the Confederate General summoned Longstreet to move on Culpeper Court House. Jackson was ordered to remain in the vicinity of the road connecting Berryville and Charlestown. Scouts were dispatched by Jackson to the Valley for the purpose of determining enemy movements.[1]

Berryville, Clark Co., November 2, 1862

I have just returned from a ride to the camp of my old comrades, with whom I have spent a very pleasant day. The old tent in which I quartered last spring and winter looked very natural, but the appearance of the regiment was very much changed. But few of the officers who were with me are in it now. In my old company I found many familiar faces in those who went with me to Harper's Ferry last spring a year ago. We then hoped a few months would end the war and we would all be at home again. Sadly we were disappointed. Many of our comrades have gone to their long home, and many more disabled for life. And now when we look to the future we seem, if any thing, farther from the end of our troubles than when they began. Many of us are destined yet to share the fate of our dead and wounded comrades, a few perhaps survive the war, enjoy its glorious fruits, and spend what remains of life with those we love. We all hope to be thus blessed; but for my part I feel that my place must be filled and my duty done, if it cost me life and brings sorrow to the dear wife and little ones who now watch my path with so much anxiety and pray so fervently for my safe deliverance. The sentiment which I try to hold and cherish is God's will and my duty to be done, whatever the future may have in store for me. I am glad to feel, darling, that although I have been writing to you for nearly eighteen months, and this has been the substitute for our once fond intercourse, I feel when I write now that I miss you none the less than I did when this cruel war first placed the barrier of separation between us. I hope as fondly as ever that the day may soon come when we will live in peace and quiet together. Eight years ago to-day, Love, we began our married life, very happy and full of hope for the future. Thus far it has been made of sunshine and shadow, joy and sorrow, strangely intermingled. The darker shade of life has for a long

---

[1] Henderson, p. 564.

time predominated; may we not hope for a change of fortune ere long?

Love, Frank

On November 6th. orders were given promoting Paxton to Brigadier-General. (See Appendix).

November the seventh was a shocking day for McClellan. He had been so confident of reaching the Southern Capital this time. The Army of the Potomac was poised for attack when he received orders from the President — not to attack but to turn his command over to General Ambrose Burnside. The President had finally heeded the General's critics and in spite of Stanton's protest — he issued the order.[2]

Camp near Port Royal, Nov. 9, 1862

The day before yesterday we had a snow, and the weather is now quite cold. Winter seems to have set in, and it finds us sadly prepared for it. A large number of our soldiers are entirely barefooted, and very many without blankets, living in the open air, without tents and with a very small supply of axes to cut wood for fires, there is much suffering. Those of our people who are living at home in comfort have no conception of the hardships which our soldiers are enduring. And I think they manifest very little interest in it. They are disposed to get rich from the troubles of the country, and exact from the Government the highest prices for everything needed for the army. I trust the Government will soon take the matter in hand, fix its own prices, and take what it wants for the army. Everything here indicates that we move to-morrow — where, there is no telling, but I trust we may soon find ourselves settled for the winter. If active operations were suspended for the winter, our men could soon build huts and make themselves comfortable. If, however, we have active operations, the sufferings of our men must be intense.

So you growl about Sunday letters. They are written on that day because all work in the army is suspended on that day and I always have leisure then. They are not interesting, you say. I am sorry for it. It is because I have but little to write about that would interest you. They always tell you I am alive and doing well. Isn't that always interesting intelligence?

You never mentioned in your letter which company White Williamson is in. Let me know and I will go to see him. Give my love to Martha, and tell her I say she has good quarters in Lexington and she had better stay there. Our army is a moving concern, and there is no telling where it will be a month hence. Possibly we may be here, quite as likely at Richmond.

You speak of the army as my idol, but you never were more mistaken. I had a good deal rather live in a house than a tent, though I can bear the change, as there is no helping it. I had a good deal rather be with you and the children that with my idol, the army, your opinion to the contrary notwithstanding. And now, Growler, good-bye.

---

[2]Henderson, p. 568, 569.

P.S. Since that was written, I have received an order conferring upon me the title of Brigadier-General and assigning me to the command of Jackson's old brigade. I made no application for it, and if I had consulted my own inclination would have been disposed to remain in my present position.

Love, Frank

Kyd Douglas was offered his old company as its commander and as he put it, "I went over the matter with Pendleton and McGuire and Paxton, my most intimate friends of the staff and then with the General," Jackson told him that since Paxton was leaving that Douglas might have more lasting experience with his company.[3]

General Paxton, having been placed in command of the Stonewall Brigade, offered Douglas the position as Brigade Inspector in addition to his position as Company Commander.[4]

Winchester, Va., Nov. 15, 1862

I left General Jackson on yesterday for my new position with much reluctance. I had with him a very pleasant situation, with work enough to keep me employed, and the society of companions I liked. I go where there is much thankless work to be done and much responsibility to be incurred. I am free to admit that I don't like the change. Yet there is no help for it. I must go, although I have changed quarters before in a happier state of mind, and with a more cheerful and refreshing prospect before me. Thirty-five hundred of my countrymen are placed under my command. If my duty be done to the best of my ability, it will not, I fear, be with such result as to give entire satisfaction. Yet if suffering or disaster spring from any act of mine, loud and deep will be the curses heaped upon my name.

How I wish that I was at home again with those who love me! It is the wish of many thousands around me who have left homes loved as well as mine. God grant it may soon be realized! But we must stay just were we are and do just what we are ordered to do. There is just no use in having will or wish in the matter, for there is nothing we can do to accomplish it. We must wait in patience for the event when the war shall end, and those of us who survive will be at liberty to return again to our old associations and pursuits. Soon we shall have winter, and it will bring with it, I fear, much suffering to our troops, and to many, I fear, a still keener pang in the letter from home telling that wife and child that never knew want before are suffering from hunger and cold. If ever a people on earth had cause upon bended knees to pray God to spare a further infliction of this terrible curse, it is ours. We have suffered much, yet the future seems to hold for us an inexhaustible store of suffering — the bloodshed of the battle, made no application for it, and the diseases which the camp and exposure engender, and the want of food and clothing produced by laying waste the country. It seems dark enough.

Love, Frank

---

[3]Douglas, p. 197.
[4]Ibid.

General Paxton expressed his official greeting to his new command in General Order No. 58. (See Appendix)

—I RODE WITH STONEWALL
Maj. Henry Kyd Douglas. Paxton's closest friend on Jackson's staff.

—VIRGINIA STATE LIBRARY
Col. Andrew Jackson Grigsby resigned when Paxton was promoted to general.

—COURTESY OF N.Y. HISTORICAL SOCIETY
A Federal railroad torn up by Jackson's men.

CHAPTER XIV

THE EXTORTIONERS AT HOME ARE OUR WORST ENEMIES

Jackson's Corps left Winchester on a blustery November 22nd. Traveling for four days the men arrived at Madison Court House where they camped for the night. As he and his men arrived at Orange Court House, thirty six miles from Fredericksburg, Jackson was informed that Burnside had reached Falmouth.[1]

On the 29th., Jackson's First Army Corps took a strong position to the rear of Fredericksburg and a small detachment was ordered to enter the city for reconnaissance. Lee began preparing for defense by fortifying Marye's Hill with adequate support for attack and counter attack. Expecting little opposition, Burnside was so surprised by Lee's preparation at Fredericksburg that he spent the next three weeks developing a plan.[2]

The purpose for bringing Jackson's Corps to Fredericksburg was to counteract Burnside's expected move toward Richmond.[3]

Spottsylvania [Spotsylvania] C. H., December 4, 1862

We have reached what I suppose to be our destination after eleven day's march stopping but once on the route. The roads were good; the troops were in good spirits, and with moderate marching reached here but little exhausted. I really don't know what we came for, as everything here is in a most profound state of quiet. The enemy are on the other side of the Rappahannock, showing but little, if any, signs of an intention to cross.

I am getting used to my new position, and, whilst I prefer that which I left, I can be contented here. I have no reason now to complain of a want of employment, but feel that I have more than I can do. I have found much that I would like to remedy, but have not the means to do it. Our soldiers are not clothed or fed now as they used to be. We are short of everything. I hope this winter that much may be supplied, and next spring we may be able to begin the campaign in fine condition.

We have bright, clear weather now, but it is the season when we may expect it not to last. Soon we shall have snow, bad roads, cold weather and the usual attendants of the season. I wish now we had the order to prepare for it and build such cheap huts as would shelter. Now very few of them have tents and many are thinly clad; some are barefooted and a few without blankets. I wish that I had the power to

---

[1] Henderson, p. 571.
[2] Ibid., p. 571, 572.
[3] Ibid.

supply their wants, but I can do but little. Have you made up your mind, Love, when the war will be over? I am heartily sick and tired of it. If any one had told me, when it began, that I would pass through two years of it and reach the rank of Brigadier, with pay of $300 per month, it would have been a flattering prospect; but I feel now as if no rank or pay could induce me to be a soldier — nothing but necessity and a feeling that I am not a true man if I leave our cause for the comforts of home? I sometimes have been severely tempted to follow the example which many whom I thought good men have set in staying at home. But other and better impulses have controlled my conduct. When we were separated in times past, I could feel with some certainty that we should be together again. Not so now. When will it be, if ever? This is the question shrouded in impenetrable gloom. I would like to see through it. I would like to know when I should be at home again to spend my life with loved wife and children. God in his mercy grant that hope so fondly cherished may some day be realized! It may never be. Yet it is a fond hope which I cherish while life lasts.

Love, Frank

*   *   *   *   *   *

Camp near Guiney's Depot, Dec. 7, 1862

We have a quiet Sunday to-day. Everything in camp stopped except the axes, which run all night and all day, Sunday included. With the soldiers it is, "Keep the axes going or freeze." They are the substitute for tents, blankets, shoes, and everything once regarded as necessary for comfort. The misfortune is that even axes are scarce; the army is short of everything, and I fear soon to be destitute of everything. It seems strange, but, thanks to God for changing their natures, they bear in patience now what they once would have regarded as beyond human endurance. Whilst I write, I expect you are sitting in our pew at church, my place by your side filled by little Mathew, — bless the dear boy! — listening to a sermon from Parson White on covetousness, avarice and such kindred inventions of Satan. I wish him success, but I fear he will hardly be able to convince — that leather can be too high, or that it is not the will of God for poor soldiers to go barefooted. God seems to have consigned one-half of our people to death at the hands of the enemy, and the other half to affluence and wealth realized by preying upon the necessities of those who are thus sacrificed. The extortioners at home are our worst enemies. If our soldiers had their sympathies, their assistance in providing the necessary means of sustaining the army, they might bear the hardships and do the work before them, feeling that it was a common undertaking for the benefit of us all and sustained by us all. But it seems like a revolution to make those rich and stay at home, and those poor who do their duty in the army.

I begin to like my new position. It occupies my whole mind and time. I begin to feel that my highest ambition is to make my brigade the best in the army, to merit and enjoy the affection of my men. I trust that both may be realized. When I came to it I knew that my appointment was unwelcome to some of the officers, but I have received nothing but kindness and respect from all. They all knew me, and knew that what I said would have to be done. I have had much better success thus far than I anticipated. We made a long march from Winchester — the longest the brigade has ever made without stopping. Usually on such marches the men fall behind, leaving the road to get provisions at the farm-houses, etc. But on this march I came very near stopping such practices. Out of the five last days of the march, on three of them every man was present when we reached the camp in the evening; on the other two days but one was missing each day. I am sure that no other brigade in the army can show such a record. During this winter I shall spend my time in trying to make them comfortable and happy, in teaching them all the duties of soldiers, and in instilling into them the habit of obeying orders. I hope to gather in all absentees, and when the winter is over to turn out at least 2500 men for duty. So, you see, Love, I have laid out my work for the winter; and you, so far, as I have said, are to take no part of my care. I think I shall be able to devote a week to you at home. I wish that week were here now, but I can't ask for it now. I must wait till the snow is deeper, the air colder. Then, I think, I will be allowed a short absence.

Love, Frank

On the 11th. of December the battle of Fredericksburg began and lasted until the 15th. Jackson sustained 3415 casualties, while the whole Confederate force received 4201. The dead numbered 458 only.[4] The Federal's counted 12,653 casualties.[5]

—*VIZETELLY*

"Prayer in Stonewall Jackson's Camp"

[4]O.R., Vol. 21, p. 562.
[5]O.R., Vol. 22, p. 97.

CHAPTER XV

I HOPE THE YANKEES
HAVE HAD ENOUGH PRACTICE
FOR THIS YEAR

After the battle Jackson hoped to return to Winchester but due to the severity of the weather he chose a spot close to Moss Neck Plantation on the Rappahannock River where he had his men prepare protective quarters for the winter.[1]

General Paxton in General Order No. 65 asked the regimental commanders to examine the conduct of the men in the recent battle. He complimented the men for their bravery but warned those who acted in a cowardly manner would be treated as such. (See Appendix)

Official reports of the battle can be found in the Appendix.

Camp near Port Royal, Dec. 21, 1862

I wrote to you some days since, informing you that I had passed through the battle at Fredericksburg without damage. The loss in my brigade was seventy six. We reached the battle-ground on Friday morning, the 12th. inst., when everything indicated that we should have a battle that day. We took first one position and then another, all the while expecting some artillery firing and some skirmishing. That night we slept in our places. The next morning all was quiet as on the day before for a while, but then the artillery and musketry became more rapid in firing, and continued to increase until for more than a mile along the line there seemed a continuous roar of musketry. We were soon ordered forward, and then I made sure we should be in the battle; but when we reached the position occupied by our second line, we were halted, and there one of my regiments became engaged with a body of the enemy which had advanced within our lines. It lasted a very little while, however. The enemy were driven back along our whole line, and not renewing it, the battle closed. That night we slept on the field, among the dead and wounded. The next morning we occupied our first line. We supposed, of course, that the battle would be renewed, but the day passed off quietly; the next day it was the same case, and the next morning it was found that the enemy had left the field and crossed over the river. We then moved down to our present camp some fifteen miles below Fredericksburg. I hear nothing from the enemy. Their pickets are on

---

[1] Henderson, p. 597.

the other side of the river, and ours are on this. When do you think we will have another battle? Where will it be? Such questions puzzle the minds of a great many people, and yours too, I doubt not. It may be to-morrow; it may not be for months. I hope the Yankees, having practice enough for the year, will conclude to go into winter quarters and let us do the same. Next week will be Christmas, and I hope a happy one to the loved wife and children of my own home. To many, in summing up and looking over their bereavements for the year, it will be sad enough. We have been more blessed, and should feel grateful for it. To the future I look, not in gloom and despondency, but with the calmness and composure of one who feels that his own destiny in a sea of troubles like this is not in any way under his control. The cloud will pass away when God in his righteous judgement wills it, and it becomes us all to bear it in patience. May the prayers which ascend to heaven from so many supplicants, with such earnestness and fervor as they never knew before, soon be answered. They will be when we deserve it.

Love, Frank

Jealousy between General William B. Taliferro and General Isaac R. Trimble erupted because each man wanted to command Jackson's old division which since Cedar Run had been under Taliaferro. When Trimble was promoted to the rank of Major General and took over the Division Taliaferro sulked. Jackson still remembered Taliaferro's part in the Romney protest and when Taliaferro began asserting undue authority while in charge of the Division it brought him into conflict with General Paxton.[2]

About two weeks after the battle of Fredericksburg, the Judge Advocate of a courts martial in the Stonewall Brigade sent the sealed findings of the court addressed to the Adjutant General of the Army to General Paxton's office for transmission forward. Paxton endorsed the communication and forwarded it to the Division commanded by Bridadier-General Taliaferro. After opening the envelope, Taliaferro returned it to Paxton with the notation that the endorsement did not conform to army regulations. Having been Adjutant General in the Jackson Brigade, Paxton felt that he had complied with them.[3]

Paxton replied that he believed a sealed communication addressed to the Commanding General of the Army should not be opened by either brigade or division headquarters and as Taliaferro had broken the seal and returned the letter it should be forwarded through some other channel. Taliaferro immediately had Paxton placed under arrest for being "very disrespectful."[4]

Lee rejected the application for a courts martial. He did,

2Vandiver, p. 443.
3Ibid.
4Ibid.

however, support Taliaferro's position rather than Paxton's.[5]

Taliaferro considering this as vindication of his part asked to be relieved of command and transferred. Lee approved the request and Taliaferro departed for duty in the Southeastern states.[6]

Camp Winder, Caroline Co., Va., January 1, 1863

I have not heard from you since the battle. Since then we have had a quiet time and everything looks like rest for some time to come. The men are fixing up their shanties for the winter. They seem happy and contented. It is sad to look back on the year just closed. We have suffered much; many good men have gone to their long home. Our loss has been 1220 in killed and wounded — more men than we could turn out for a fight to-day. Out of the fifteen field officers elected last spring, five have been killed and six wounded, leaving only four that have escaped unhurt. In these losses are many whom we were always accustomed to regard as our best men. I published to-day an order naming our camp, which gives some facts of our history, and I send you a copy of it.

How are the matters at home? In the excitement of active work, I have too much to do to harass myself with idle dreams of home; but now since we are at rest I cannot keep my mind from it. I feel there is nothing which I would not give to be with you for an hour or a day. I could have gone home and have spent a couple of weeks when I received my appointment, before taking command; but I really thought the brigade was sadly in need of a commander, and that it was my duty to stay. Now I am fixed and must apply for leave just as any private in the ranks. I know it would not improve my standing with my superior officers to ask for a leave, but still I feel very much tempted to do it. If the snow falls deep, and we have such severe weather as to preclude the possibility of active work, my homesick malady may get the better of me. I would like to see you, Mathew, Galla and the baby. Have the children forgotten me? It seems so long since I saw them.

Just here an officer calls who says he comes upon the disagreeable duty of placing me in arrest by order of Gen. Taliaferro, who regards a communication which I sent him today as very disrespextful. Very good; there is a small chunk of a row to be settled, which I shall do in that calm breaking the seal and returning the paper, it would be sent to its destination through some other channel. Perhaps he differs with me upon the point, and thinks I meant to be offensive. So much for this piece of news. Now, darling, I will bid you good-night.

Love, Frank

Upon being arrested, General Paxton placed Col. Funk in charge of the brigade. After a week Paxton returned to the brigade.[7]

Paxton named the encampment Camp Winder in honor of the

---

[5]Lee To Jackson, Headquarters, Army of Northern Virginia, Jan. 12, 1863, in Taliaferro papers, Box 1, William and Mary College Library.

[6]Ibid., p. 444.

[7]Freeman, p. 505.

previous brigade commander and officially described Winder's courage in Brigade General Order No. 1. (See Appendix)

From the 9th. through the 16th. of January men of the Paxton's Brigade were doing picket duty along the Rappahannock River with their newly issued rifles from Austria. During one of the lighter moments on the 15th. General Paxton gave a dinner for his staff which consisted of such delicacies as wild goose, oysters, and scrambled eggs. [8]

Camp Winder, January 17, 1863

We returned yesterday from a week's tour of duty on picket, and the men are now camping in their old camp. We had very good weather, with the exception of one day's rain; and it was cloudy and seemed every day as if bad weather was coming upon us. Whilst there I got an order to cook one day's rations and be prepared to move at any time. But several days have elapsed and no order yet to move. I think it is very improbable that such an order will come before spring. The Yankees, I doubt not, are having a quiet time in winter quarters, and, I think have seen enough of us to last them until spring. Appearances indicate an engagement in North Carolina. It is probable they will make an effort to take possession of the railroad and of Wilmington. If so, we will have, I doubt not, a severe battle there. I expect, too, we shall hear of another attack on Vicksburg before long. So far as we are concerned here, I feel, perhaps, too confident. We have whipped the army in front of us very often, and I feel sure that we can do it any time. We repulsed their attack at Sharpsburg, where, I am sure, we did not have more than half of our present strength. I do not think their army can ever be increased, but the symptoms of dissatisfaction at the North must tend largely to diminish it. Our independence was secured in the last campaign when we proved our capacity to beat the finest army they could bring in the field. The war may be protracted, there is no telling how long; but we have shown our capacity to beat them, and we are better able to do it now than ever before. But many of us may never live to see the end; it may last long enough to see the end of more of us than will be blessed in living to see the end of it. If it be God's will that my life shall be lost in it, I feel that I should await my fate contented, if not with cheerful satisfaction. The next world we must all see sooner or later, and in this business one must make up his mind to look upon the change with composure. Every sense of fear and alarm must be controlled in such a way that he may act free from the influence in the midst of dangers which at other times would have made him shudder. It is well that we cannot know to-day the events of to-morrow; that upon the eve of our pain and death we may be made happy by the anticipation of pleasure which we are destined never to enjoy. So, darling, I live upon the hope that this war may some day end, that I may survive it, and that you and I may spend many a happy day together. God grant that it may be so!

I had hoped to have gotten home this winter, but I think there is no chance of it. My only hope for a furlough is to get shot or get sick. This is the misfortune of my promotion. Before I could go and come

[8]Douglas, p. 206.

when I pleased, but now I am fixed while the war lasts. Now, Love, I will bid you good-bye. Write often.

Love, Frank

The Union troops trying to maintain composure in this time of despair were being tormented by the constant rain. Burnside decided to attack and ordered his men to the river with the intention of crossing one of the fords. Men were sinking up to their knees in mud as they tried to maneuver into position and the cavalry was instructed to dismount and have each man use his animal to carry supplies. When the wet troops reached the United States Ford on the 21st., Burnside ordered a frontal attack.[9]

The order caused havoc within the Union ranks. General William B. Franklin stormed into headquarters shouting that New Jersey had just elected a Democratic senator and that such an order might cause his troops from that state to rebel and if they did fight and lose a number of men the state might withdraw from the war. Burnside laughed and told him to leave his headquarters. Sumner, who had just joined the pair, argued with his commander and Burnside commanded, "Silence, the attack will be made in the morning." Other Generals began forming with the group and Hooker agreed with Franklin that his men would probably refuse to fight.[10]

The storm of protest gathered momentum and Hooker dispatched one of his brigadiers to Washington to plead with Lincoln to stop another Fredericksburg. Burnside visited the President with the request that Hooker be replaced for incompetency and cowardice. Lincoln, heeding the demands of Hooker and others, told Burnside that he need not return to the army. After their removal, the president passed over Sumner and Franklin to appoint Hooker causing the by-passed generals to go into retirement.[11]

Camp Winder, January 25, 1863

I spent yesterday in bed, and feel to-day like getting back into it. Whilst I have not lost any time from sickness since I last left home, I have been often unwell and compelled to lie in bed for a day or two. A few days' quiet generally bring it on again. I never was better than when I came to the army last summer; but about the time of the battle of Cedar Mountain it began, and has continued, making me often hardly fit for duty. It is in some measure owing to a want of vegetables and fruit, and to bad bread. The next opportunity I have, I will send to Richmond and get a stock of crackers, dried peaches, etc.

We have occasionally had an alarm, but generally everything has

[9]Pratt, p. 164.
[10]Ibid.
[11]Ibid.

been quiet. Yesterday morning we had an order to send our extra baggage to the rear, but it arose, I believe, from the accidental bursting of a shell in Fredericksburg, which set the armies on both sides to beating the long roll. My brigade has been rapidly increasing in the last month by the return of sick and absentees. I hope by spring to bring it up to 2200 present, and to have it in a high state of efficiency. Then I expect some good service from it.

You say you have forty-eight barrels of flour at the lumber-house. After saving for your own use what you want, get Wm. White to send off the balance and sell it. Have the balance of the wheat ground, so that you may get the offal, and send off the flour. I wrote you in my last letter a good deal about the farm. Let me hear in your next letter all about them. I have but little time now to think of them, and trust it all to you. If my work here is well done, it will occupy my whole time. I should like to fill my place here, so as to leave it with some credit to myself. To do this will leave me but little time for matters on the farm. So you must be housekeeper, overseer, man of all business, and everything. You may as well learn now, and if you will devote your mind to it you will have no trouble. With such assistance as you can get from Matt and your father, you will be able to get along very well.

When I was lying in bed I half wished that I might get sick, so that I might get home for a little while; but I think my disease is destined to take an unfavorable turn so as to deprive me of that pleasure and keep me in camp.

Give my love to little Matthew and Galla, and tell them I say they must be good boys, and do everything you tell them. How I wish that I could be with you again! I hope the day may not be far distant. This hope is the last thing with which I wish to part. Now, darling, good-bye. Write often.

P.S. After closing and sealing up my letter, I break it open to say that I received yours of the 17th. inst. It is sad, Love; but still I am glad to know that I am prized at home even by the baby. God bless him, and — a more fervent prayer still — may he teach me my duty! Just here the Chaplain comes to say that the two of my poor soldiers condemned to die desire that their remains may be sent home, and my answer was that all in my power should be done to further their wishes. How I wish that I had some place where less responsibility was thrown upon me! May God give me strength to meet in the spirit of mercy and justice. How sad it is to think of the distress which this punishment must bring upon others! It makes me shudder to think of such a fate being brought upon the wife and children of my own household. I feel in no humor, Love; I am too sad to write anything which would please you.

Love, Frank

General Paxton's illness took the "favorable turn" which he hoped for, and conditions became such that a brief leave of absence became necessary, and he spent a few weeks with his family.

During the first week of February the men of Paxton's Brigade built a small chapel of pine logs. Paxton attended several services later in the small church accompanied by Jackson.[12]

Camp Winder, February 20, 1863

I have been improving since I got back to camp, and now begin to feel that I am quite well. I trust that it may continue, for during the last six months I have suffered much from the fact that I have seldom been very well.

Until this morning we had snow and rain continually since I returned. This is a bright, clear morning, with a strong wind, which I think will soon dry the ground. As it is now, the roads are so muddy that it is next to impossible to get provisions for our men or feed for our horses. Since I reached camp I have been quite busy. The day before yesterday I wrote eight pages of foolscap paper, more than I have written in one day for the last two years. I sometimes think if my health were good my eyes would give me no trouble.

There is an impression that a large part of the force which was in front of us has moved. If so, it indicates that we, too, before many days may move, and that there will be no more fighting on the Rappahannock. In three or four weeks we will have spring weather, and then we may expect employment. Where we will be in a month hence, God only knows. Some of our troops have already moved, but their destination is not known. It is a business of strange uncertainties which we follow. For my part, I have gotten used to it, — as an affliction with which despair and necessity have made me contented. I used to look upon death as an event incident only to old age and the infirmities of disease. But in this business I have gotten used to it as an everyday occurance to strong and healthy men, some upon the battlefield and others by the muskets of their comrades. Four of my brigade have been sentenced to be shot — three for desertion and one for cowardice. It is a sad spectacle, and I sincerely wish that their lives might have been spared. I trust that God in his mercy may soon grant us a safe deliverance from this bloody business. Such spectacles witnessed in the quiet of the camp are more shocking than the scenes of carnage upon the battle-field. I am sick of such horrors. If I am ever blessed with the peace and quiet of home again, oppression and wrong must be severe, indeed, if I am not in favor of submission rather than another appeal to arms. I came away from home without your miniature; send it to me.

Love, Frank

The court martial mentioned in the letter had also sentenced two other men to be flogged. Paxton wished to lessen the sentence of the condemned men and he asked that only one be shot and the others be given life imprisonment. He further requested that the men's sentences be decided by lots. Major Trimble, the adjutant, approved the request and forwarded it to General Jackson.

Jackson, before sending it to Lee, wrote the following:

With the exception of this application, General Paxton's management of his brigade has given me a great deal of satisfaction. One great

---

[12]Douglas, p. 207.

difficulty in the army results from over lenient courts and it appears to me that a courts martial faithfully discharges its duty that its decisions should be sustained. If this is not done, lax administration of justice and corresponding disregard for law must be the consequence. The army regulations define the duty of all who are in service and departures from its provisions lead to disorganization and inefficiency, . . .[13]

Lee studied the matter for two days and then concurred with Jackson's findings due to the fact that the cases had been carefully tried, "however painful it may be to inflict the severe punishment which the good of the service requires."[14]

When General Paxton received the communique with its endorsements and comments he bowed to the weight of authority and handed it to Douglas, his adjutant, with the comment, "The sentence must be executed, you must attend to it."[15]

On March 2nd., the day set for execution, President Davis pardoned the men.[16]

—*BATTLES AND LEADERS*
Jackson's attack on the right wing of the Federals at Chancellorsville.

[13]Douglas, p. 213.
[14]Ibid.
[15]Ibid.
[16]Ibid.

CHAPTER XVI

TO SUCH MEN DEATH IS NO ENEMY

Camp Winder, March 8, 1863

To-day I went to our chapel to hear Dr. Hoge, who preached a very fine sermon, Genl. Jackson being one of the audience. We have preaching in the chapel twice on Sunday, and, I think, pretty much every night. It looks odd to see a church full of people, and all of them men. It would be really refreshing to see a woman among them, to give the audience the appearance of civilization. But the women and children who adorn our churches at home are missing here. Well they may be! I am glad, at least, that mine are not here to share the miseries of this business with me.

During the past week it has been a blow or rain, a hurricane or a shower, all the time. The wind seems to dry up the ground, taking the water up somewhere, and it is no sooner up than down it comes again.

In army matters we have the most profound quiet. It has been so long since I have heard a musket or a cannon that I have almost forgotten how it sounds. I suppose, however, in the course of a month we will have something to refresh our memories and revive old scenes. Yes, we will have the long roll to warn the men that another battle is imminent; then the solemn march to the scene of the conflict, each pondering upon the misty future; then we are halted and our line of skirmishers thrown to the front; then we have occasional shots, which gradually thicken and extend until there is one continual roar of musketry and artillery; and, perhaps, to close the scene, we lie down exhausted to sleep upon the field, among the dead and dying. You civil people at home all look upon this as terrible. So it is, but we soldiers must get used to it; each waiting in patience for his time to fall among those who rise no more for the contest.

Give my love to Lou [his wife's sister] and say to her that Mr. Newman's regiment is now at Fredericksburg; that I will send up to him and let him know to-morrow that his box is at the depot; and that I will write to an officer from my brigade who is on duty at the depot to take charge of it until he sends for it. I was very sorry, indeed, that I was not able to bring the other box with me.

I have had more to do of late than usual, and have sometimes spent four or five hours at my writing-desk — not, however, without some pain in my eyes when I quit work. I am able to keep pretty well when I live on rice and bread, but if I eat a hearty meal it puts me out of order again. I hope by care to keep fit for duty, but do not expect to get well until I get a better diet and am able to lead a more regular life. I heartily wish that I were right well. It gives me much anxiety lest, when my services are most needed, I shall prove unfit for duty and be compelled to leave my brigade in charge of some one else.

Love, Frank

*   *   *   *   *   *

I will devote a part of this quiet Sunday evening to a letter home. Our camp looks to-day like it was Sunday. We stop our usual work when Sunday comes, and, like Christian people, devote it to rest. To-day I attended our church and listened to a very earnest and impressive sermon from one of our chaplains. He is one of the best men and best chaplains I ever knew. He devotes his whole time to his duties, and remains all the time with his regiment, sharing their wants and privations. I am sorry to say we have few such in the army. Many of them are frequently away, whilst others stay at houses in the neighborhood of the camp, coming occasionally to their regiments.

To-day I had a visit from the father and mother of a poor fellow who has been tried by a court martial for cowardice. She was in great distress, and said it would be bad enough to have her boy shot by the enemy, but she did not think she could survive his being shot by our own men. I gave her what comfort I could, telling her his sentence had not been published and there was no means of knowing that he was sentenced to be shot; that if it turned out to be so when the sentence was published, she could petition the President for his pardon; that he was a good man and would pardon her son if it was not an aggravated case. I pitied her, she seemed so much distressed. I heartily wish this sad part of my duties were over. I have about twenty of my men in close confinement, whose sentences have not been published, many of whom are condemned to death. It is for Gen'l Lee to determine what shall be done with them.

Whilst I write the sleet and hail are falling fast, accompanied by frequent claps of thunder, cold and chilly withal. Winter, it seems, will never end. Last week it was all the while a severe wind and freezing cold. I really don't care much now how long it lasts. I do not wish to move from here until spring is fairly opened. My men are comfortably fixed here, and when we move the huts must be left behind, and, besides this, most of the blankets sent off, as we have no wagons to haul them. My men, I fear, when we move will have to get along with such clothing and blankets as they can carry. Many of our horses have died this winter for want of forage, and those that remain are much reduced in flesh and strength.

I have received your miniature, reminding me of times when you and I were young; of happy hours spent, a long time ago, when I used to frequent your parlor in the hope that you might be what you now are, my darling wife. Then the present was overflowing with happiness, the future bright and beautiful. We have seen much of each other, much of life, its joys and sorrows since then. By the grave of our first child we have known together the deep sorrow of parting with those we love forever. In this long absence of two years, we have felt the sadness of a separation with such chance of its being forever as we did not dream of when we began life together. May God in his mercy soon bring us together in our dear home, never to separate again, to spend what of life is left to us in peace and happiness.

Love, Frank

On March 16th. Jackson moved his headquarters from Moss Neck to Hamilton's Crossing which lay within ten miles from Fredericksburg.[1]

---

[1] Douglas, p. 210.

Camp Winder, March 22, 1863

I am grateful to you for the tender interest in my health manifested in your last letter, received some days since. For the last week I have felt better than I have before this winter. I have gotten a half-bushel of dried peaches from Richmond, and, living upon these for the most part, I have improved very much. I am so much pleased with the medicine that I think I shall send to Richmond and get another bushel. So, I think, you may give up your idea of a furlough.

It commenced snowing again on Thursday evening, and snowed or rained all day Friday and Saturday. To-day the sun is shining brightly, the birds chirping, and some signs of spring again. I hope now we may have good weather, and that you may be able to make some speed with your farm work.

I had an unexpected visitor at my tent yesterday evening — Mr. Junkin of Falling Spring Church. I divided my bed with him, and did what I could to make him comfortable. He has special claims upon my hospitality as the pastor of my old church. It is associated in my mind with many loved friends who have now gone to their long homes, and from it I derived my earliest impressions of the church and the pastor. Twenty long years have passed since I used to go there to church. I have grown that much older, but I fear not much wiser or better. I remember and reverence the teachings of my venerable pastor, but have not made them the guide of my life as I ought to have done.

I laid aside my pencil and paper just here to go over and hear a sermon from Mr. Junkin. It was impressive and eloquent. When he alluded to our missing comrades of the last campaign, there was a solemn stillness, and many eyes moistened with tears. It is sad, indeed, to think how many good men we have lost. Those upon whom we all looked as distinguished for purity of character as men, and for gallantry as soldiers, seem to have been the first victims. I never saw an audience more attentive than our soldiers are at church. The great mass of them are good men, who have not lost in the army the habits which they learned in their churches at home. I like to see those whose lives may be spared to return home without being contaminated with the vices of the army.

Love, Frank

In the following letter Paxton appears to have a premonition of death. Within five weeks he would be dead.

Camp Winder, March 31, 1863

You will have, in your troubles on the farm, much to try your patience. My advice to you is to bear it all in good temper, to know all that is going on; and by devoting your mind to it you will find that you succeed much better than you anticipate. There is no work so profitable in one's business as thinking about it. I have always found that when I was interested in what I had on hand, and thought much about it, that I found some good and easy plan of accomplishing what I wanted to do. I have, as you know, short as my life has been, followed all sorts of trades. I' have been lawyer, banker, farmer, soldier, etc., and any success which I have met with I ascribe to the thinking which I have devoted to the business. You, I doubt not, have found the same about your housekeeping. Now apply this to the farm, and you will have an easy time.

Whilst I value your love as the best treasure which I have on earth, I would not have you harass yourself with a painful anxiety about my fate. The thread by which I hold my life is brittle, indeed, and may be severed any day. I have thought much of it, and think that I feel content to accept whatever fate God's justice and mercy has in store for me; and my prayer is that he will give me such faith, repentance and conformity to the law of his holy Gospel as is required of the sinner. I feel that I can say, "If it be possible, let this cup pass from me; but thy will be done." Sooner or later I must drink it, and if it be God's will that it be now, I am content. Sooner or later I must die, and, if prepared to die, my life can never be given to such a cause as that in which it is now staked. I may survive the dangers before me; many thousands will. If such be the will of God, I trust his law may be the guide in what remains for me of life. Sooner or later, darling, the ties which bind me to you and the children of our home must be severed forever. If I be the first to go, and the charge devolve upon you, teach them, as the experience of their father's life, that there is no honor on this earth save in the path which God's Word points out for the humble and contrite Christian. Outside of this there is no success in life, no wealth or distinction which does not bring wretchedness as the reward for the labor which it costs. Perhaps there may be many years of happiness in store for us, dark and bloody as the future may seem. May God in his mercy end the struggle!

Love, Frank

* * * * * *

Camp Winder, April 12, 1863

Your letter of April 7th. came to hand yesterday, bringing the welcome intelligence of all well at home. I will spend part of this quiet Sabbath in writing to you in answer to it. It is a very pleasant and warm April day, — so pleasant that our log church has been abandoned and the chaplains had service in the open air. I witnessed to-day what I never saw before; the sacrement administered in the army. It was, indeed, a solemn and impressive scene; a congregation composed entirely of men, standing around in a circle of which the chaplain was the center, receiving the bread and wine in renewal of their vows and fellowship as Christians.

A number were admitted for the first time to the sacrement, and received into the church. The whole assembly wore such an air of seriousness and devotion as I have seldom witnessed before. There was no excitement, but an exhibition of earnest devotion in the discharge of the highest duty on earth. Far away from wife, mother and sister, separated from them perhaps forever in this world, they met, this mild April Sabbath, in the open air, some of them for the first time, and others to renew their sacramental vows of faith in Christ and fresh exertion to deserve his mercy. Men like these, however gloomy the future may be, look to it pleasantly and happily, contented to receive whatever of good or ill God has in store for them with the supplication, "Thy will be done!" Relying with implicit faith upon his mercy, the future is stripped of its gloom and becomes all bright, beautiful and happy. To such men death is no enemy, but a messenger expected from God sooner or later, and welcome as the quick path to a holier and happier life. With such soldiers in our army and such men at home, we might bid defiance to all the boasted numbers and strength of our enemies and feel sure of victory. But it is sadly true that the mass of our men here and at home are not of this type. Very many of our officers and soldiers — very many more, I think, of our people at home — have grown worse instead of better by the calamity which has fallen upon us. It is strange that it should be so; that our depravity grows deeper and darker in proportion to the severity of affliction. How little we know of the future! Last Sunday I thought another week could not pass without more blood. The reasons which prevented it during the winter — the weather and the roads — no longer exist. We have for some days had good weather and good roads, and no reason why the enemy should not advance, if so disposed. I place but little confidence in my judgement as to what will happen; but I have rather come to the conclusion that the enemy does not mean to attack us here. There is nothing which seems to indicate an advance. I am inclined to believe we have nearly as many men at our command here as they have opposed to us, and I think it likely they know it.

Their balloons go up every day, and from these they have a full view of the location of all of our troops; I suppose we shall have some activity after a while. If they do not move, we shall, I think. Whenever the struggle comes, I feel sure of success — that God will bless us with another signal victory. We have a just cause and a splendid army, and I trust that our next engagement may be attended with such signal success that much will be accomplished towards closing the war. I look to the future with much confidence. Many of us must go down in the struggle, never to rise again. Such may be my fate. Sometimes I try never to let my hopes fix upon anything beyond this war, such is the uncertainty of surviving it. Then I find myself happy in the dream and hope of the time when it will all be over, and I shall be with you again, to spend the rest of life in peace and quiet. God will that it may be so! If not, I am content. Sooner or later we must separate in this life, and it will be whenever God so wills it. Despondence and despair under such circumstances is foolish and sinful. Far better to be contented and complaisant, ready to do our duty and submit in patience to our fate, whatever it may be.

And now, darling, good-bye. Give my love to Matthew and Galla, and a kiss to little Frank. Write often, and believe me, dearest, ever yours.

Frank

Mrs. Jackson and her daughter visited the camp on April 20th. — the daughter Jackson had not seen. They spent some happy hours at Mr. Yerby's house which lay about a mile from camp.

While Mrs. Jackson and young Julia were there, many men of the corps paid their respect. This was the last time Mrs. Jackson saw her husband before she was called to his deathbed.[2]

Camp Winder, April 20, 1863

I received your welcome letter of the 15th inst. on Saturday. I am very sorry to hear that Jack is still unfit for work, and that Phebe, too, has taken sick. Bear it all in patience, and do the best you can. Pay almost any price rather than not get one. If you get behindhand with the work, you will not soon get it up.

As to C., I can't be far wrong. He is not as bad as you think he is; but even if he cheats me out of the whole crop, it would be better than to leave it idle. Somebody, and certainly the country, will get the benefit of the crop, if we do not. As to the pay for grazing Mr. _____'s cattle, you are right; say nothing to your father about it. I would rather lose the price than have an unkind feeling about it. I have a strong aversion to having any business transactions with my kin, as they are so often the cause of ill feeling.

I have been waiting for nearly a week for a fair day to change my camp, and moved this morning, hoping to have sunshine for one day at least to fix up. But I have been unfortunate. I had hardly reached the new camp before the rain commenced, and my men, I fear, being poorly provided with tents, have suffered much from it. My old camp, I thought, from the accumulation of filth during the winter, was the cause of an increase of sickness among the men. I hope now, as we have a good supply of spring water and clean ground, that the health of the men will be better. I have hardly ever known the army so quiet as now. We had every reason to believe that as soon as the spring opened the enemy would advance and we should have a great battle, in which I anticipated a splendid victory, but heavy loss. Three weeks of spring have passed, and so far from an advance, there is every indication that there will be none. So, too, all along the line. There seems no disposition on the part of the enemy to hazard an advance. How different the future now from this time last year! Then the enemy was pressing at every point, and all was gloomy for us. Now it is all bright and prosperous. If we wait for activity here from the enemy, we will, I think, remain in this camp all summer. The prospect is not so cheering when we look within our lines. Christian people have forsaken the God of their fathers for the sake of money, an idol worse than images of metal or stone.

The President's patriotic appeal, I see, is answered by the committee of one county: "Hay, twenty cents per pound"; by that of another: "Wheat, $6.50 per bushel." I do not believe there is such a scarcity as to justify such figures, but the famine is of Christian charity and public spirit. Men wish to grow rich upon the miseries of their country, and there is no limit to their extortions. All seem holding back what they have in the hope that a starving army will raise the price of bread and meat still higher. God will give us the blessing of independence and peace fully as soon as we deserve it; and our prayer should be now not so much for victory to our arms as for patriotism and charity to our people, wisdom and integrity to our

---

[2]Douglas, p. 211, 212.

rulers. The depravity of mankind is alike the great truth and great wonder of the universe. These times seem to develop it in a degree of monstrosity which we could never have supposed it would obtain.

And now, darling, good-bye. Give my love to dear little Matthew and Galla, and kiss little Frank. May God bless and take care of you all!

Love, Frank

*   *   *   *   *   *

(No date, first page of letter being lost. It was probably April 27, 1863)

We had a snow here on Saturday night which continued yesterday morning and is now about gone. The roads are now in pretty good condition, and if the enemy wish to make the attack, there is, I think, no reason now for deferring it on account of the roads. But, darling, there is no telling when it will be. The future, ever a mystery, is more mysterious now than ever before. Our destiny is in the hands of God, infinite in his justice, goodness and mercy; and I feel that in such time as he may appoint he will give us the blessings of independence and peace. We are a wicked people and the chastisement which we have suffered has not humbled and improved us as it ought. We have a just cause, but we do not deserve success if those who are here spend this time in blasphemy and wickedness, and those who are at home devote their energies to avarice and extortion. Fasting and prayer by such a people is blasphemy, and, if answered at all, will be by an infliction of God's wrath, not in a dispensation of his mercy.

The future, as you say, darling, is dark enough. Though sound in health and strength, I feel that life to many of us hangs upon a slender thread. Whenever God wills it that mine pass from me, I feel that I can say in calm resignation, "Into thy hands I commend my spirit." In this feeling I am prepared to go forward in the discharge of my duty, striving to make every act and thought of my life conform to his law, and trusting with implicit faith in the salvation promised through Christ. How I wish that I were better than I feel that I am; that when I close my eyes to-night, I might feel certain that every thought, act and feeling of to-morrow would have its motive in love for God and its object in his glory! Well, so it is. Why is it we cannot feel sure that the sins of the past are never to be repeated? May God give me strength to be what I ought to be — to do what I ought to do! And now, darling, good-bye. When we meet again, I hope you will have a better husband — that your prayer and mine may be answered.

Love, Frank

Thus, Frank Paxton wrote the last letter to his wife.

CHAPTER XVII

HE HAD A PREMONITION
OF DEATH

TELEGRAM

May 3, 1863

The enemy was dislodged from all his positions around Chancellorsville and driven back towards the Rappahannock, over which he is now retreating. We have to thank Almighty God for a great victory. I regret to state that Gen'l Paxton was killed, Gen'l Jackson severely and Gen'l Heath [Heth] and D. H. Hill slightly wounded.

(Signed) R. E. Lee
Gen'l Commdg.

* * * * * *

President Davis,
Richmond, Virginia

May 3, 1863

Yesterday General Jackson penetrated rear of the enemy, and drove him from all his positions from the Wilderness within 1 mile of Chancellorsville. He was engaged at same time in front by two divisions of Longstreet. This morning the battle was renewed, and enemy driven from all his positons around Chancellorsville, and driven back toward Rappahannock, over which he is now retreating. Many prisoners were taken, and the enemy's loss is heavy in killed and wounded. We have again to thank almighty God for a great victory. I regret to say that General Paxton was killed, General Jackson severely wounded, and Generals Heath and A. P. Hill slightly.

R. E. Lee
Commdg. Gen'l.

On Sunday May 3rd., Major Kyd Douglas came to the field hospital with news of the Stonewall Brigade. At each note of bravery General Jackson brightened.

"The men of that brigade," Jackson told McGuire at his cot, "will be, some day proud to say to their children, 'I was one of the Stonewall Brigade.' "

Smith told him in answer to a question about losses and of the death of Paxton.

"Paxton? Paxton," he said in disbelief.

"Yes sir, he has fallen," Smith told him.

The General turned his face to the wall, closed his eyes, and lay long in silence. Then he spoke seriously and tenderly of Paxton's virtues. Smith also said Paxton had a strong conviction that he would be killed. "He gave minute instructions for such an event, and read calmly and devoutly from his New Testament just before advancing," Smith explained.

Jackson listened and then said about his friend's preparation for death, "That's good, that's good."[1]

Letter from Henry K. Douglas to Mrs. Paxton
May 4, 1863

Madam:

As the senior officer of Gen'l Paxton's staff, and a person with whom he was probably more intimate than with any one in the brigade, I deem it my duty, although a painful one, to notify you of the circumstances of his death. He fell yesterday morning while bravely leading his brigade into action, and lived only an hour after receiving the wound. As soon as he was struck he lifted his hand to his breast-pocket. In that pocket I knew he kept his Bible and the picture of his wife, and his thoughts were at that moment of heaven and his home. Beloved and esteemed by officers and men, his loss is deeply mourned, and the brigade mingle their tears with those of his family relations.

I have for some time thought that the General expected the first battle in which he led his brigade would be his last, and I had observed, and am satisfied from various conversations with him, that he was preparing his mind and soul for the occasion. It is a consolation to know that while he nobly did his duty in the field and camp without regard to personal consequences, he had been convinced that there was a home beyond this earth where the good would receive an eternal reward. For that home he had richly prepared himself, and, I confidently hope, is there now. Almost the last time I saw him, and just before the brigade moved forward into the fight, he was sitting behind his line of troops, and, amidst the din of artillery and the noise of shell bursting around him, he was calmly reading his Bible and there preparing himself like a Christian soldier for the contest.

Dr. Cox, A. D. C., has already departed with his body for home.

* * * * * *

Letter from Henry K. Douglas to J. G. Paxton
Hagerstown, Md., Feb. 18, 1893

Yours of the 14th. is received to-day. I knew your father very well, When he was on the staff of Gen'l Jackson, so was I; and for a time, when he commanded the Stonewall Brigade, I was the A. A. G. and A. I. G. of the brigade, in rank its senior staff officer. My relations with him were very close — indeed, confidential.

---

[1]Dabney, p. 709.

I had observed, during the winter of 1862-63, a growing seriousness on his part in every respect. There was nothing morbid about it, but he was much given to religious thought and conversation. He was a very regular reader of the Bible, and, I think, often talked with Gen'l Jackson on the same subject. He was thoroughly impressed with the conviction that he would die early in the opening campaign, and was determined to prepare for that fate.

In my letter to your mother, written the day after his death, I merely alluded to certain conversations which I will now explain more explicitly.

The night of the 2nd., Gen'l Paxton seemed — as we in fact all were — very much depressed at the wounding of Gen'l Jackson. Late that night, in the course of a conversation with me, your father quietly but with evident conviction expressed his belief that he would be killed the next day. He told me where in his office desk certain papers were tied up and labelled in regard to his business, and asked me to write to his wife immediately after his death. I was young and not given to seriousness then; but I was so impressed with his sadness and earnestness, and all the gloom of the surroundings, that I did not leave him until after midnight.

The next morning we we astir very early. I found Gen'l Paxton sitting near a fence, in rear of his line, with his back against a tree, reading the Bible. He received me cheerfully. I had been with him but a few minutes when the order came for his brigade to move. He put the Bible in his breast-pocket, and directing me to take the left of the brigade, he moved off to the right of it. I never saw him again. I find, in looking for some time before I knew it, and that I was commanding the brigade by issuing orders in his name long after his death. When I knew of it, I informed Col. Funk, who immediately assumed command. I mentioned in the letter to your mother that he lived an hour after his wounding. Capt. Burton says this is an error, and it probable he is correct. I was not with Gen'l Paxton when he was shot, and I suppose that what I stated in my letter was obtained from some one else. Capt. Barton was with the General. I find this in my notes: "I missed Gen'l Paxton and the rest of the staff; but as I missed part of the 2nd. Regiment, I thought it and the General had become temporarily separated from the rest of the Brigade." I find in my notes of the 4th.: "I wrote a letter to Mrs. Paxton concerning the death of the General." This is the letter a copy of which you sent me, and I am very glad to get it.

Gen'l Paxton was a unique character. He was a man of intense convictions and the courage of them. Kind-hearted, he was often brusque to rudeness. He was conscientious in the discharge of his duties, and painstaking. He was of excellent judgment, slow and sure, and yet fond of dash in others. He was esteemed by the officers, beloved by the men, and respected by all. He was an excellent officer, a faithful, brave and conscientious soldier. He had a keen sense of humor, well restrained, and often laughed at and condoned recklessness of which he did not approve. I think I must have tried him often; but if so, he never let me know it. I had his friendship, and in all his friendships he was staunch and true.

P.S. I find this in the account of my interview with Gen'l Jackson on Sunday evening, the 3rd: "He spoke feelingly of Gen'l Paxton and Capt. Boswell, both dead, and his eyes filled with tears as he mentioned their names. He asked me to tell him all about the movements of the old brigade. When I described to him its evolutions: how Gen'l Paxton was reading his Bible when the order came to advance; how he was shortly afterwards mortally wounded; how Gen'l Stuart led the brigade in person shouting, "Charge, and remember Jackson!" etc., etc., his eyes lighted up with the first fire of battle as he exclaimed, "It was just like them — just like them!"

*   *   *   *   *   *

Letter from Randolph Barton to J. G. Paxton
Baltimore, Md., Sept. 14, 1885

My recollection is that in the summer or September of 1862, your father, who up to that time had been a member of the staff of Gen'l Jackson (Stonewall), was by that officer appointed to the command of the Stonewall Brigade, — Gen'l Winder, its last commander, having been killed at Cedar Mountain.

I was a brevet second lieutenant in Co. K, 2nd Va. Infantry, Stonewall Brigade, during the winter of 1862-3, and your father was at that time acting Brigadier Gen'l. Early in 1863, upon the recommendation of Mr. Henry K. Douglas, your father detailed me to act as Assistant Adjutant Gen'l of the brigade, and about March or April, 1863, I left my company and went to his headquarters. A little later the Confederate Congress confirmed his appointment as Brigadier-General, and there-upon, although he did not positively tell me that he wished me to remain with him permanently, he suggested that I should supply myself with a horse, which I took as a hopeful sign of my promotion.

My impressions are not clear, at this length of time, as to your father's religious life during the period immediately preceding the opening of the campaign of 1863, but I am sure he daily read his Bible, and on Sunday went to the Brigade's religious services, held in a large, rude log house, in which I remember distinctly to have seen Gen'l Jackson with great regularity.

On the afternoon of May 2, 1863 about three o'clock, Gen'l Jackson's command completed the flank movement which placed him in Hooker's rear. Your father's brigade brought up the rear of the column, and as it emerged from the dense pine forest and blinding dust upon the Plank Road leading from Orange C. H. to Chancellorsville and Fredericksburg, Gen'l Jackson halted it, allowing the rest of the column to go on, and for some moments, seated on a fallen log back in the woods, engaged your father in earnest conversation.

Gen'l Jackson then rejoined his column, your father formed his brigade across the road, about evenly divided by the road, and with his staff advanced down the road some few hundred yards. After a while firing commenced on the left, and one of us was dispatched by your father to bring up the brigade in line of battle, which was done, and by nightfall we had resumed our position at the right of Gen'l Jackson's line. The enemy had been completely surprised by the advance on our left, had fled in great confusion, and our brigade had been very slightly engaged.

We spent the early hours of that night on the roadside, or in shifting positions. Finally, about one o'clock the next morning, we got into the line of battle not far from the enemy. Our rest was constantly broken by volleys of musketry, and we all knew that daybreak would usher in an awful conflict. I was close to your father all this time, as my duty required, and recall now with vivid distinctness the fact that he was dressed in a handsome gray suit, which had only a day or so before been received from Richmond, having on its collar the insignia of a .Brigadier-Gen'l. Perhaps the wreath was not on the collar, only the stars, — one of your father's characteristics being aversion to display. By the very first dawn of day, when with difficulty print could be read, your father opened a Bible, a very thick, short volume, probably gilt-edged, — read for some time, and as the sound of approaching conflict increased, carefully replaced it in his left breast-pocket, over his heart. In a few moments a tall officer from Gen'l Stuart, who had succeeded Gen'l Jackson, hurried us to the right of the road, and we were immediately engaged in a terrific battle. Our brigade had faced the enemy and were slowly advancing, firing as they advanced. I was within a foot or two of your father, on his left, both of us on foot, and in line of our men. Suddenly I heard the unmistakable blow of a ball, my first thought being that it had struck a tree near us, but in an instant your father reeled and fell. He at once raised himself, with his arms extended, and as I bent over him to lift him I understood him to say, "Tie up my arm"; and then, as I thought, he died. Some of our men carried him off, and after a while, being wounded myself, I went back, passing his body in an ambulance.

Official records describing Frank Paxton's and his brigade's activities at Chancellorsville can be found in the Appendix.

—GENERALS IN GRAY

GEN. ELISHA FRANKLIN PAXTON

CHAPTER XVIII

IT IS WELL WITH THEE

Letter from A. C. Hopkins, Chaplain, 2nd, Va. Infry. to Mrs. Paxton.

Near Richmond, May 12, 1863

In the tenderness and freshness of your grief, you may deem me an intruder, though I come to sympathize with you. Esteem for your husband while living, and regard for his memory now that he is removed from earth, prompt me, a stranger, to send you this letter.

I am a chaplain of his former command. An attack of typhoid fever caused me to be removed from camp to a kindly roof in the vicinity some six weeks ago; and from there I was rapidly hurried off from a sick-bed to avoid capture just the day before my admired General's death. Of course, therefore, I could not be with him on that ill-fated day, and have nothing of his last words to send you for comfort. I know, however, he died as a brave, patriotic soldier, whose home and family are invaded and humiliated by an enemy, would prefer to die, doing his duty for their defence. With all this you have been made more fully acquainted than I have, and therefore I leave it.

I can boast no claim to the special confidence of your husband. What I tell you, you may have learned before from his own pen or tongue. But I am assured that you will be much comforted to learn that in every conversation with me for months past he has given evidence of very serious reflection on the subject of religion; and so great has been his zeal in encouraging chaplains in the religious instruction of his troops, that I am induced to hope that the blood of Christ had purchased his soul, and he is among the rejoicing saints in light.

During my illness he kindly came to see me twice, the last time but a few days before the battle, and each time he introduced and continued to speak on religious matters. He always proved himself the chaplain's warm friend so long as he endeavored to promote the spiritual interest of his regiment and proved faithful to his ministerial office.

Now, madam, please accept the tender sympathies of a friend, admirer and member of your lamented husband's former command, although a stranger to you. May the great Comforter administer to you all the consolation which Heaven bestows on earth, and be so good a Guide and Light to your fatherless children as to compensate for their great bereavment. My failing strength bids me cease. With kind regards and tenderest sympathies for you and your mourning household, I am your sincere friend.

Elizabeth Paxton survived her husband long enough to implant in the hearts of his three sons a devotion to the memory of their scarcely remembered father which remained to them an inspiration throughout their lives. The growth of the man during the period of his war letters was the striking feature of them. With great natural courage and burning patriotism he went forth almost joyfully to the conflict. With growing seriousness he passed through the horrors of battle after battle, until we find him in that winter camp in the Wilderness. There his heart was filled with sadness unutterable as he saw about him all the miseries of war. He had in many battles looked death in the face without fear, but now it was death looking him in the face. His own soul-conflict was upon him, and with his other struggles he was wrestling with God. During the two years of service the youthful enthusiasm had vanished, and in its place had come heroic determination. The man who wrote those last letters would not have turned one hair's breadth from the path of duty to have saved his life. In that wilderness near Chancellorsville, on the night of May 2, 1863, there came to him his Gethsemane. To his trusted staff officer he says, ''I shall die to-morrow.'' The night is spent in marching and countermarching, and daybreak finds him reading his Bible. This done, he gives the command that puts his brigade into action, and takes his place in the center of his brigade, in the line with his men, a position of as great danger as any of his command. Within a few minutes, at about seven o'clock, the death summons came, and he fell to rise no more. It was not his to be with his men through their glorious charge and victory. A modest tombstone in the quiet graveyard at Lexington marks his resting-place, and bears the simple inscription: ''It is well with thee.'' If to be faithful unto death, to willingly lay down one's life for an ideal, entitles one to peace and rest in the great hereafter, then, Christian soldier, it is well with thee!

JOHN GALLATIN PAXTON
Son of General Paxton

APPENDIX

OFFICIAL RECORDS AND CORRESPONDENCE PERTAINING TO E. F. PAXTON

Sunday, September 14, 1862
C. S. Army of Operations about Harper's Ferry, W. Va.

"My signal flag was up at sunlight, and my glass bearing on Loudoun Heights after sunrise. Major Paxton sent the following, 'Artillery coming up the road to be repaired.' Before delivering the message I asked, 'What artillery and what road?' Major Paxton answered, 'Walkers, and up the mountains.' About 10 A.M. comes another dispatch from Loudoun Heights. 'Walkers, six rifle pieces in position. Shall he wait for Mc Laws?' General Jackson answers, 'Wait.' "

J. L. Bartlett
Captain[1]

Headquarters V District
September 23, 1862

General:

I respectfully recommend that Major E. F. Paxton be appointed Brigadier-General and assigned to the command of the Brigade lately under Brigadier-General C. L. Winder. Last year he was major of the 27th. Regiment of the brigade and ranked all the officers at present in the brigade except three. Upon the reorganization of the Volunteer Regiment, Major Paxton was not retained. As he served under me in the line, and at various times I assigned important duties to him, and as for several months he has been my A. A. General, my opportunities for judging of his

---

[1]O.R., Vol. XIX, p. 959. The island referred to was one in the Shenandoah River below Harper's Ferry.

qualifications have been remarkably good; and there is no officer under the grade proposed whom I can recommend with such confidence for promotion to a Brigadier-Generalcy.

I am, General, Your obedient servant,
T. J. Jackson, Major General[2]

October 27, 1862
Hqs. Army of Northern Virginia

To Honorable George W. Randolph, Secretary of War
Richmond, Virginia
From Robert E. Lee

Major E. F. Paxton is recommended to be promoted brigadier-General to command Winder's Brigade.[3]

Special Order No. 234 from A. P. Mason, Asst. Adj.
General 2nd. Corps.
November 6, 1862

Major E. F. Paxton, Assistant Adj. General to be Brigadier-General to command Winder's Brigade.[4]

Major Paxton
Asst. Adjutant-General

Major General Steuart has relieved my cavalry in Winchester and I am operating now in the country in every direction. In a scout upon the Pughton Road yesterday I brought in 150 stragglers found loafing in the various farm houses. Today I sent to Clarke County, to Pughston, toward Romney, toward Front Royal, and expect to make a sweep, as the country is full of stragglers. I have sent back already 5,000 or 6,000. The provost guard is as of no assistance, and little was doing. The labor has been constant, but I hope it has been repaid by a gratifying increase in the army. The number of officers back here was most astonishing. After due notice, I ordered the cavalry to arrest and bring to the rendezvous all officers, as well as men, found in the rear without proper leave. It created quite a stampede in the

---

[2]*Memoir and Memorials — Elisha Franklin Paxton*, p. 97, Compiled and Edited by John Gallatin Paxton, Printed, Not Published, 1905.
[3]O.R., Vol. XIX, p. 683.
[4]O.R., Vol. XIX, p. 698.

direction of the army. I hope to clear the rear sufficiently by Monday to enable me to return to my command. There are about 1,200 barefooted men here. I am satisfied that a large number throw away their shoes in order to remain. If barefooted men are permitted to remain here, the number will continue to increase, this should if possible be remedied.

Very Respectfully,
J. R. Jones
Brigadier General[5]

Indorsement
Hqs. Army of Northern Va.
September 29, 1862

Respectfully submitted to the Secretary of War for his information.

R. E. Lee
General[6]

General Order No. 58
Headquarters Paxton's Brigade, Jackson's Division
2nd. Corps
Camp Baylor, Va., November 18, 1863

The Brigadier commanding, assuming the position, embraces the opportunity to express his appreciation of the honor received in being assigned to a brigade which, by its valor, in the first conflict with the enemy won for its General a name which his virtues and the achievements of his troops have made immortal. Under the lead of Jackson, Garnet, and Grigsby, who with you had shared and survived the perils of battle, under Winder and Baylor, who have fallen in front of your lines and are now mourned among your gallant dead, you have gathered laurels which he trusts may not hereafter be suffered to wither upon your standards.

He hopes to merit your good opinion by his efforts to provide for your comforts and promote your efficiency, and by his participation with you in all the dangers and all the hardships of the service.

He expects that such example as he may set, of attention to

---

[5]O.R., Vol., XIX, p. 629, 630.
[6]Ibid.

duty and obedience to orders, will be followed by the officers and men of his command.

(Signed) E. F. Paxton
Brig. Genl.
(Signed) E. Willis,
Capt. & A. A. A. Genl.

General Order No. 65
Headquarters Paxton's Brigade
December 18, 1862

Regimental commanders will institute a close examination of the conduct of officers and men in the late battle. They will see that merited censure and punishment falls upon delinquencies; that fidelity and gallantry are rewarded with praise and promotion. If any remained behind in camp or fell to the rear without proper leave upon the march, which seemed to all to lead to the field of battle, or when brought to the enemy sought safety in flight, their officers will see that they are arrested and the proper steps taken for their punishment.

Your line, as it moved after long hours of weary suspense to the support of your comrades in front, exhibiting the spirit and determination of soldiers resolved to conquer or die, was witnessed by your brigade commander with a feeling of pride and gratification such as he had never known before. Such a result can never be achieved by men who harass themselves and alternating hope of safety and fear of danger; it is the work only of the soldier who habituates himself to the idea that he must stand to his colors so long as he has a cartridge or a bayonet to defend him; and if he fails in this he deserves to be despised and cast off even by the women and children of his own home. He who moves under such a resolution must of necessity do his duty, win the applause, and a still nobler reward in the conviction which it causes to his own heart that he is the meanest feels he would like to be — a true man and a true soldier.

He who proves recreant to his country and his cause at such a time merits the just sentence of military law — to die under the colors he disgraced and by the muskets of the gallant comrades he deserted.

E. F. Paxton
Brig.-Gen'l

Official
    Friend C. Cox, A.D.C.

The following extracts were taken from the official records of the Union and Confederates Armies, Series I, Vol. XXI, — Fredericksburg:

REPORT OF BRIG. GEN. E. F. PAXTON, C. S. ARMY, COMMANDING FIRST BRIGADE

Hdqtrs. Paxton's Brigade, Jackson's Division,
Camp near Corbin's Farm, December 24, 1862

Captain: In pursuance of the order from division commander to report the participation of my brigade in the battle near Fredericksburg, I have the honor to state that my brigade, consisting of Second, Fourth, Fifth, Twenty-seventh, and Thirty-third Virginia Regiments and Joseph Carpenter's battery, numbering in all about 123 officers and 1100 men, marched from its encampment, near Guiney's Depot, on Friday morning, the 12th. inst., at day-break. After reaching the battle-field and making frequent changes of position, when the engagement commenced my brigade occupied a position near the crest of the hill some four hundred yards in the rear of General Gregg's brigade of A. P. Hill's division, my right resting on the left of Ewell's division. My orders were to support General Gregg, and be governed in my actions by his movements. Upon a report from my orderly Mr. F. C. Cox whom I had sent forward to obtain information that Gregg's battery was moving, I ordered my brigade to the front in line of battle. About the time of reaching General Gregg's position, the Second Virginia Regiment, occupying the right of my line, came in view of the enemy, and under the order of Capt. J. Q. A. Nadenbusch, commanding the regiment, filed obliquely to the right and rear, but scarcely effected its change of position when it was fired upon by the enemy. Expecting, from the indications, that my troops would be engaged in this position, I proceeded to bring forward the Fifth and Fourth at double-qqick and post them upon the right of the Second, and to put the Twenty-seventh and the Thirty-third Regiments in position upon its left. These dispositions, however, were not accomplished until the firing ceased, the enemy having been gallantly repulsed by the Second Regiment. Soon after I changed my position and occupied the military road. While there I found that troops were falling back in disorder past the right of my line, when I deemed it prudent to move some three hundred yards to the right upon the road, to guard against an advance of the enemy in that direction. Again I changed position and occupied the line of the fence in front.

That night my brigade slept on their arms on the military road, and the next morning, before daylight, in pursuance of an order from the division commander, took position on the railroad, my right resting opposite the position which my left had occupied on the military road. Here the day passed off quietly, with the exception of occasional firing between the pickets.

Carpenter's battery was detached from my brigade on the 12th. inst. and was not under my orders during the engagement. A report of its participation in the engagement, by Lieutenant [George] McKendree, commanding, is transmitted herewith.

I am much indebted to my regimental officers — Captain Nadenbusch and [R. T.] Colston, acting field officers of the Second Virginia Regiment; Lieutenant-Colonel [R. D.] Gardner, and Major [William] Terry, Fourth Virginia Regiment; Lieutenant-Colonel [H. J.] Williams and Captain [J. W.] Newton, Fifth Virginia Regiment; Lieutenant-Colonel [James K.] Edmondson and Major [D. M.] Shriver, Twenty-seventh Virginia Regiment; and Colonel [Edwin G.] Lee, Thirty-third Virginia Regiment — for the exhibition of great gallantry, skill and coolness in the discharge of their duties.

Lieutenant-Colonel Gardner, after having passed unhurt and distinguished for his gallantry through all the battles of the campaign, — Port Republic, Richmond, Cedar Mountain, Manassas, and Sharpsburg, — fell, at the head of his regiment, severely, if not fatally, wounded.

To Adjt. C. S. Arnall, Fifth Virginia Regiment, acting as my assistant adjutant-general, the highest praise due for his gallant and energetic discharge of the duties incident to the position.

To the rank and file of my command I am especially grateful for the courage, fidelity and promptness exhibited in obeying my orders. My brigade sustained a loss of killed, 4; wounded, 69; missing, 1 Total, 74.

*   *   *   *   *   *

REPORT OF BRIG. GEN. WM. B. TALIAFERRO
COMMANDING JACKSON'S DIVISION
Camp near Moss Neck, Va., December 24, 1862

Captain: In comformity with the order of the Lieutenant-General commanding, I have the honor to report the operations of this division on the 13th. and 14th. instant, before Fredericksburg. On the morning of the 12th. ...... I posted Paxton's and Starke's (Pendleton's) brigades in rear of Gregg's and Thomas' of Hill's division, and held Taliaferro's and Jones' brigades in reserve . . . Early on the morning of the 13th. . . . General Paxton, finding that our troops were giving back to the right of Gregg's brigade, and the enemy advancing beyond the front line through a gap which fronted a boggy wood supposed to be inaccessible to the enemy, moved his brigade to the right and engaged with two of his regiments the enemy, who had penetrated to the military road, but who were retiring by the time he reached that point. He then pushed forward to the front, and occupied for the rest of the day the front line at that place . . . I take pleasure in stating that the officers and men behaved admirably, displaying coolness and courage under fire, and changing positions without any disorder or confusion. I would particularly mention Brigadier-Generals Jones and Paxton . . . I enclose a list of killed and wounded, amounting to 190.

* * * * * *

REPORT OF BRIG.-GEN. JUBAL A. EARLY
COMMANDING EWELL'S DIVISION
December 27, 1862

Captain: I have the honor to submit the following report of the operations of this division in the action of the 13th. instant, near Fredericksburg . . .

Seeing this brigade falling back, I halted it on the hill in the woods immediately in the rear of the place at which it had first met the enemy, and caused it to be reformed under the command of Col. C. A. Evans of the Thirty-first Georgia Regiment; and fearing that the enemy might follow through the same interval with a fresh column, I sent to General D. H. Hill for reinforcements, and he sent two brigades forward. Before, however, they arrived, Brigadier-General [E. F.] Paxton of General [W. B.] Taliaferro's division had filled the interval left open by the falling back of this brigade by promptly moving his own brigade into it.

General Orders No. 1.
Headquarters Paxton's Brigade
Camp Winder, January 1, 1863

In memory of the gallant officer who led the brigade at the battles of Winchester, Port Republic and Richmond, and whose valuable life was lost at Cedar Mountain, the present encampment is called Camp Winder. In the losses of the year just closed, twelve hundred and twenty killed and wounded, you have much to mourn. The eye moistens with an unbidden tear to find that many of the officers whom your free choice had appointed to lead you, of the messmates and comrades you loved, are missing now. On Richmond, Manassas, or on some other field of carnage, they have met a soldier's fate and found a soldiers grave. In its achievements you have much cause for pride. You have marched fifteen hundred miles, encountering the snows and ice of winter in the mountains of Morgan and Hampshire; the heat and miasma of summer in the swamps of Henrico and Hanover. You have met the enemy in nine severe battles, and in all, save one, God has blessed your arms with victory. You have the proud satisfaction of knowing that you have participated in the campaign which has given your country a brilliant name in history, and that you have contributed with your blood to its success. To-day you begin another year in the service of your country, and in the achievement of its independence. God speed you in your glorious work! You began the campaign but twelve hundred muskets — a small number, it is true, but borne by men inured alike to the dangers and hardships of the service, who will make up in hardy courage what they lack in numbers. Imitate the valor of Winder, Allen, Baylor and Neff, and you have a brilliant future before you.

(Signed) E. F. Paxton
Brig. Genl.

Official. Friend C. Cox, A.D.C.

The following extracts are taken from the official records of the Union and Confederate Armies, Series I, Vol. XXV, — Chancellorsville:

REPORT OF BRIG.-GEN. E. E. COLSTON, C.S. ARMY, COMDG. TRIMBLE'S DIVISION
May 2, 1863

The First Brigade, under General Paxton was detached from the division and ordered to report to Brigadier General Fitz Lee of the cavalry. This brigade was not engaged during the evening of the 2nd., and did not rejoin the division until the next morning.

Early on Sunday morning orders were given to the division to form at right angles to the Plank Road near the Log House occupied as a hospital by the enemy. Colston's and Jones' brigade on the right of the road and Paxton's and Nicholl's on the left, in second line.

By this time the enemy was advancing in very strong force toward the right of our line and of the breastworks, and were about outflanking us on the right. Seeing the danger, I sent Mr. Grogan of Gen. Trimble's staff, to order Paxton's Brigade to move by right flank across the road.

This was a most critical moment. The troops in the breastworks, belonging mainly (I believe) to General Pender's and General McGowan's brigades, were almost without ammunition and had become mixed with each other and with the fragments of other commands. They were huddled up close to the breastworks, six and eight deep.

In the meantime, the enemy's line was steadily advancing on our front and right almost without opposition until I ordered the troops in the breastworks to open fire upon them. At this moment Paxton's Brigade, having moved by the right flank in line of battle, advanced toward the breastworks. Before reaching them, the gallant and lamented General Paxton fell. The command devolved upon Colonel [J. H. S.] Funk, Fifth Virginia Regiment. The brigade advanced steadily, and the Second Brigade moved up at the same time. They opened fire upon the enemy and drove them back in confusion . . .

I cannot, however, close this report without mentioning more particularly, first, the names of some of the most prominent of the gallant dead. Paxton, Garnett, and Walker died heroically at the head of their brigades.

* * * * * *

REPORT OF COL. J. H. S. FUNK, 5TH. VA. INFANTRY, COMDG. PAXTON'S BRIGADE

Captain: I have the honor of submitting the following report of Paxton's Brigade in the late operations around Chancellorsville:

The brigade under the command of Brig. Gen. E. Frank Paxton, composing the 2nd., 4th., 5th., 27th., and 33rd., Va. Regiments, left Camp Moss Neck on the morning of April 28th., marching to Hamilton's Crossing, where we bivouacked.

We remained at this place until daylight on May 1, when we took up the line of march in the direction of Chancellorsville, in Spotsylvania County, and reaching the Plank Road leading from Orange Court-House to Fredericksburg, about 6 miles from the latter point, we halted until near sunset.

At this time the firing on our front became quiet heavy and rapid, and the brigade was ordered forward. We pushed forward some distance, to within a mile of our advancing line, where we bivouacked for the night. As night approached, everything became once more quiet on the front.

On the following day, at dawn, we continued the march down the Flank Road, and, arriving at the point at which Generals Anderson's and McLaws' division were in position awaiting the approach of the enemy, we turned abruptly to the left by a road but little used, leading by Catharine Furnace to the Brock Road. We marched down this road to Germanna Junction, where General Paxton was detached from the division and ordered to report to Brigadier-General Lee of the cavalry, who placed the brigade in position at this point, extending across the road. I have not been able to learn the nature of the instructions received by General Paxton. We remained here until unmasked by the troops in our front, when we moved forward in line of battle through the woods, perhaps 1/4 of a mile, and then by the flank on the Orange Road until 1-1/2 miles of Chancellorsville, where we again formed in line of battle along the enemy's breastworks, our right resting on and the line at right angles with said road.

At 11 pm the brigade was ordered to take position on the right of the road and about 200 yards in advance of our former position. We remained here for two hours, when we were directed to take another position on the left of the Plank Road a half mile in advance, our left resting on said road and in second line of battle. As soon as the lines were connected, the men, worried and worn out by the rapid detour made that day and by want of rations, were permitted to rest for a few brief hours.

On the morning of May 3 (Sunday) we were aroused at daylight by the firing of our skirmishers, who had thus early engaged the enemy. At sunrise the engagement had become general, and though not engaged, and occupying the second line, the brigade suffered some loss from the terrific shelling to which it was exposed.

At 7 A.M. we were ordered to move across the Plank Road by the right flank about three hundred yards, and then by the left flank until we reached a hastily constructed breastwork thrown up by the enemy. At this point we found a large number of men of whom fear had taken the most absolute possession. We endeavored to persuade them to go forward, but all we could say was of little avail. As soon as the line was formed once more, having been somewhat deranged by the interminable mass of undergrowth in the woods through which we passed, we moved forward. Here Paxton fell while gallantly leading his troops to victory and glory.

Many valuable officers and men were killed or wounded in the faithful discharge of duty in the assault of Chancellorsville and the following is the statistics for the battle:

Paxton's Brigade
List of Killed or Wounded

	Killed	Wounded	Total
Brig. Gen. E. F. Paxton	1		1
2nd. Virginia	8	58	66
4th. Virginia	14	149	163
5th. Virginia	7	113	120
27th. Virginia	9	62	71
33rd. Virginia	10	56	66
Total for Brigade	49	438	487

SELECTED BIBLIOGRAPHY

PRIMARY SOURCES
Books

Dabney, R. L., *Life and Campaigns of Lieut-Gen. Thomas J. Jackson.* New York, Blelock Co., 1866.

Douglas, Henry Kyd, *I Rode With Stonewall.* New York, Fawcett World Library, 1961.

Jackson, Mrs. Mary Anna. *Memoirs of Stonewall Jackson.* Louisville, Prentice Press, 1895.

Johnson, Robert Underwood & Clarence Clough Buel (eds.). *Battles and Leaders of the Civil War* (4 vols.). New York, Century, 1887.

Newspaper

Lexington (Va.) *Gazette,* August 8, 1861.

Manuscripts and Unpublished Works

Judiah Hotchkiss Collection, Library of Congress, Manuscript Division.

Memoir and Memorials — Elisha Franklin Paxton. John G. Paxton. Independence (Mo.), Privately Printed, 1905.

Taliaferro Papers, Box 1, William and Mary College Library.

SECONDARY SOURCES
Books

Chambers, Lenoir. *Stonewall Jackson* (2 Vols.). New York, William Morrow & Co., 1959.

Freeman, Douglas S. *Lee's Lieutenants* (3 Vols.). New York, Chas. Scribner's Sons, 1944.

Henderson, Col. G.F.R. *Stonewall Jackson and the American Civil War.* New York, Longman, Greer & Co., 1961.

Robertson, Jas. I., Jr. *The Stonewall Brigade.* Baton Rouge, LSU, 1963.

Vandiver, Frank B. *Mighty Stonewall.* New York, McGraw-Hill, 1957.

INDEX